spin

your sugar

like naked yarns

the world

your only dye

Spin

Taking Your Creativity to the Nth Degree

claire burge

illustrated by brian dixon

T. S. Poetry Press • New York

T. S. Poetry Press
Ossining, New York
Tspoetry.com

This book includes various references from or to the following brands and sources: Vaseline, Unilever; Sunlight Soap, Unilever; Evernote, Evernote; "Mending Wall," by Robert Frost, *North of Boston*, Henry Holt and Co, 1917; "Managing Motivation to Expand Human Freedom," by David C. McClelland, *American Psychologist*, 33(3) 201–210, 1978; Artist Date is a concept from *The Artist's Way,* by Julia Cameron, Jeremy P. Tarcher/Putnam, 2002; Marmite, Unilever; *The Famous Five Series*, by Enid Blyton, Hachette UK, 1942; Weekly Blueprint Concept, Get Organised; Master List Concept, Get Organised; Wunderlist, Wunderkinder; any.do, any.do.

Some names have been changed to protect the privacy of individuals.

Illustrations and cover image by Brian Dixon

ISBN 978-0-9898542-1-4

Library of Congress Cataloging-in-Publication Data:
Burge, Claire
[Self-Help/Creativity.]
Spin: Taking Your Creativity to the Nth Degree/Claire Burge
ISBN 978-0-9898542-1-4
Library of Congress Control Number: 2013948774

for Dad,

who taught

me

HOW

to **bite** INTO *Life*

My SUGAR CANE

LAURA: FOR BELIEVING IN UNDISCOVERED VERSIONS OF ME.

CALVIN: FOR ALLOWING MY WILD ♡ HEART TO BE JUST THAT, WILD.

JO: FOR RAISING THE BAR WITHOUT EVEN KNOWING IT.

MRS MAAS: FOR WRITING THAT COMMENT ACROSS THAT VERY FIRST ESSAY AND HELPING ME TO SEE HOW MAGNIFICENT A WELL CONSTRUCTED SENTENCE IS.

BETH, GEORGIA, SHEILA,

SONIA: FOR PUSHING ME TO BE MORE ALWAYS.

OLIVE SHOAN COOKS: FOR YOUR GENES; WOVEN IN TO MINE.

BEE: FOR FINDING MY TRUE SUGAR YARNS.

EVERYONE WHO ANSWERED MY TWO QUESTIONS ABOUT CREATIVITY OVER FACEBOOK: I HOPE YOU ARE DELIGHTED AND SURPRISED. YOU ARE HERE.

MOM COOKS: FOR TREATING MY LIFE LIKE A CUP OF TEA THAT NEEDS TO BE ENJOYED FROM FINE BONE CHINA.

LESLIE: FOR OUR SABBATH MORNING VOICE NOTES. YOU KNOW. YOU JUST DO.

MONNA: FOR ASKING THE HARD QUESTIONS.

BRIAN: BECAUSE THIS REALLY IS YOURS AS WELL; I HOPE THE RISK WAS WORTH THE PROCESS

KENDALEE, NADIA: FOR BEING THE VERY FIRST READERS I REALLY CONNECTED WITH ALL THOSE YEARS AGO; BECAUSE OF YOU I STARTED TO TAKE MY CREATIVITY AND MY WORDS MORE SERIOUSLY.

TRACEY: FOR ACCOUNTABILITY; I WOULD BE NOWHERE WITHOUT IT.

SAM: FOR TEACHING ME THE ART OF REWORKING WORDS AGAIN AND AGAIN.

ANN: FOR BRINGING TO LIGHT THE BEST VERSION OF THESE WORDS. THOROUGHNESS IS YOUR ART.

CLIFFORD, MATTHEW, THE CATS, THE DOLLS And SHARLIE BEAR: FOR RIPENING MY IMAGINATION. LET'S INVENT A TIME MACHINE AND GO BACK?

Table OF CONTENTS:

1 • IT STARTS Somewhere

It all starts with a book in a bathroom.

A younger version of me starts writing thoughts about the day-that-was, in a journal that lands in my bathroom. A visiting friend decides to risk being found out for snooping. He writes me a letter in the back of it. Another friend also opens the pages and adds her thoughts somewhere in the middle. Along the line, Mom and Dad realise this is a window into teenaged mayhem and ink their love, too. My boyfriend's mom decides to do the same.

And so, the book comes to live in the magazine basket just outside the shower. Water-splattered and slightly misshapen from condensation, the pages quickly fill with wisdom I don't want to lose.

I am falling in love with the conversation happening on pages that never go beyond the door. I start a shorthand version in another book. I call it shorthand because instead of labouring over details, I simply pen the lessons I am learning—most of them painful, and I'm fully bent on not experiencing them again.

I number these shorthand lessons and the book grows, in parallel to the more conversational one in the bathroom. The only difference is the shorthand lessons are my very own.

I leave school, finish two degrees, hitch myself to a boy, catch a jet plane with a one-way ticket, find a house on a hill, start a business and another business, buy a bike, fall off the bike, and all along the way I pen the lessons. Each time, I ink the page and read through previous entries, remembering the moments. When difficult situations crop up, I go back, look at lesson #63, #89, #103 ... #7, #18, #33 and connect some dots that weren't obvious before.

I had written lesson #733 when Laura called and asked if there was a book in there. I said I thought there was.

So here I am back at the bathroom book, with the story-behind-the-story.

I haven't discovered a creativity formula that I am hypothesising about. This is a collection of practical moments: snapshots of a girl living curiously, but still not curiously enough.

I hope you will find yourself somewhere in the story and leave your own note. I'll look for it in the bathroom basket.

2 • Meet Brian

I only needed two things as a child: a pen and paper. I would draw for hours—creating characters, imagining fantastical scenes, reliving recent experiences. On the page, my young mind willed a second world into being.

As I grew up, I never grew out of this habit; I held onto it as a core part of my identity and pursued visual communication as a career. I loved studying design at college, especially entering a system that emphasised mindfulness and attention to craft, so different from the rigid curriculum and examinations I had previously known. However, it took me a while to fit in. Unlike some students, my mind seemed incapable of exploring alternative possibilities or producing multiple visions on request. I was cautious back then. Literal. Although I could draw, I wasn't very creative. As you will find out in this book, one doesn't necessarily follow the other.

A turning point occurred in college, when I realised that if I wanted to pursue a career in graphic design I would have to adjust. I began to take chances with materials, concepts, and methods. Slowly I discovered the transformative power of sketching out ideas, viewing sketchbooks as more than white space to be filled up; they became places to embark on visual adventures. By the time I graduated, not only had the standard and quality of my work changed, but I, too, had adopted a heightened sense of awareness.

After working as a graphic designer in Dublin, I embarked on a year-long journey of self-discovery. Traveling had always been my ambition, but I had no specific plan. I wanted to do certain things, like visit India and volunteer at an organic farm in New Zealand. During that year, I saw

those sites and performed the tasks, but people stood out most of all. So many wonderful individuals crossed my path, offering their thoughts, laughter, and countless snippets of wisdom.

At first I struggled with how to respond to these kindnesses and inspirations. Then I began sketching the experiences and sharing the art with others. People responded gratefully. On a street in Calcutta one day, I felt compelled to draw a doorway I noticed. A small crowd of schoolboys encircled me. They seemed surprised to find me drawing nothing but a doorway, but they continued to watch. Together we shared the experience of seeing details emerge on the page that might have gone unnoticed. Most people enjoyed being included and finding something they could recognise among the eclectic scribbles. I made friends. I fell in love. Country by country, city by city, creativity enabled exchange.

Illustration—or drawing, if you like—is now central to my work as a design practitioner and researcher. Even if a project doesn't require hand-drawn visuals, chances are I will still need to "sketch it out." Showing something, rather than just saying or writing it, is often the most effective means of conveying a message. At least that's what I've found.

I hope you enjoy this book, and my contribution to it (the illustrations). In terms of advice, if it's creativity you're after: engage with the world. Look outward as well as inward. Balance the two. For me, this is where creativity is found: in that beautiful, brilliant space called *being*.

What You Will find in this Book:

• 3

?? Questions that will get you thinking creatively

?? Questions about your own approach to creativity

T Practical tips on making creativity part of daily life

→ Practical tips on → scheduling → creativity into the everyday life

Stories of moments that defined a creative life

Life lessons learned living a creative life.

PICTURES that make all the words come alive

A HEART

What YOU CAN DO WITH This Book

4 •

Use it upside down

Use it the RIGHT way up

Make art WITH IT.

DOODLE WHATEVER COMES TO MIND

Make it your own

Record YOUR OWN thoughts

Write on it

Give it Away

keep it AS A JOURNAL

share it WITH PEOPLE WHO IGNITE YOUR CREATIVITY

Tell Claire & BRIAN WHAT you think of it

Allow it to CHANGE you

Read only the STORIES

SKIP TO THE EXERCISES AND FOCUS ONLY ON THE QUESTIONS.

WORK THROUGH THE BOOK FROM BEGINNING TO END

A → B

CHANGE YOURSELF WITH IT

Discover MORE of yourself in it

Tell others About it

Argue WITH it

.... Other

What I hope You Do with this Book

• 5

All of the Above/previously/aforementioned

and more . . .

IT SHOULD LOOK UNIQUELY YOURS After YOU'RE Done with it.

6 • Smoky Blankets and Safety Pins

Creativity Needs a safe place

"she picks me up and lovingly flings me over her shoulder"

The morning begins when Mom kisses me goodbye before going to work and hands me over to Margaret whose rough chocolate hands plonk me onto the bed before she picks me up and lovingly flings me over her shoulder, so I am positioned at the base of her ample bottom. She throws a smoky blanket around the both of us, pulls it tight under me and makes a big knot in the cleft of her voluptuous breasts. She fastens it with a heavyweight safety pin. Forget the high chair. I have a better view, and it is constantly changing.

The alto of her voice beats against my chest. She hums a low, deep sound. Sometimes the notes are happy, light. Sometimes each sound strains from within her, and she mourns as she sings. Sometimes she whistles for good measure. It is then that her hips sway, too, and I bob like a cork at sea.

I see the world from many angles this way. Sometimes I look at it sideways when I bury my head into her back and close my eyes, feeling the rough felt texture of the blanket scratching against my cheek. Sometimes I look left to right as I push away from her back and lean into the tightly wrapped blanket. When she stoops low to pick up toys and washing, I see the world upside down. The trees are more playful from this angle: their fluffy tufts look like gigantic mops that need to sweep the dark earthen soil at their bases.

I hear Dad's car in the driveway, the creaking open of the garage door. When his large frame bumps through the doorway, his face is strained, grey. He asks Margaret to take me off her back; she does so reluctantly, eyeing him. Dad picks me up and explains that Mom is very sick, that they have to cut a piece of her throat out because it has gone bad. I look at the rotting orange in the fruit bowl and he nods his head:

"Yes, like that, and the doctor needs to take it out and throw it away."

"Is Mommy going to die because her throat is only half now?"

"We don't know, but as soon as we do, I promise to tell you."

I flee to my room. I am turning 'round and 'round, moving from my toy box to my bed then to my cupboard where I climb inside.

Margaret finds me there, pulls me out roughly. She is agitated, muttering in Zulu. I don't know what she is saying, but many years later I come to understand that in Zulu culture you never take a child off her mother's back when she is distressed. Never.

She bends down low again. I am mounted and safety-pinned in. She goes outside and finds things to do, many things that will keep her hips swinging. She sings low, mourning with me. I fall asleep and when I wake up, I am warm against the heat of her body. I watch the driveway as my mom's car makes its way forward. Margaret unfastens me, carries me over, and transfers me to my next place of safety.

"Are you going to die, Mommy?"

"I don't know, but we are going to eat lots of vegetables so that I don't, and the doctor is a good doctor, which means that he will do everything to not let me die. "

"Okay, Mommy."

Six years later i am again fleeing, this time up the steep driveway, away from a tumour in my mom's brain. Margaret is waiting for me at the door. I am too big to be flung onto her back and safety-pinned in. Instead, I bury my head into her warm chest. My insides erupt and I hiccup in pain. She sings low, her hips swaying, pulling me gently this way, that way.

At 19, I am in another cupboard trying to breathe deeply the smell of Dad. I know that it will grow fainter every day as his body returns to dust. I long for Margaret. I want to be roughly pulled from this cupboard, told that everything will be okay in low humming sounds with swaying hips.

IN PURSUIT OF CREATIVITY:

1. WHERE DID YOU HIDE AS A CHILD?
2. What places of safety have you created for yourself now?
3. DOCUMENT situations in which you have felt unsafe and unprotected. DOCUMENT what brought a sense of safety amidst the turmoil.

"creativity NEEDS a place to kick off its shoes"

"...in Zulu
culture
you
never take
a child off
the mother's back
WHEN Distressed.
Never."

7 • Bed on Bricks

Creativity NEEDS the unfamiliar

"she explains that the tokoloshe *comes at night and if her bed is on bricks, he can't reach her"*

Like a granular, somewhat-translucent white volcano, it *putt-putt-putts* away in the enamel pot on the stove. Margaret refuses to use the good pots, saying they're not "burned-in" like her pot. It seems ready to me, but according to her it needs to *putt-putt-putt* like that for at least 40 minutes, to allow the ground maize to absorb all the water, swell, and become her staple food. She calls it *pap*. I watch closely, peering over the rim of the lopsided pot as it shifts uneasily on the hot rings. It is as if the *pap* is breathing, in and out, in and out. She swats me to the side, tells me I will get burned and then she will be in trouble.

I look up into her black eyes: those beautiful dark circles surrounded by white, that remind me of my ebony marbles—the heaviest ones that I prize most of all. Her skin is shiny because of the Vaseline® she rubbed onto it that morning when she was getting ready for work; it is smooth and smells so familiar to me. It is my comfort. I bury my head in her apron, which is stained with silver polish and tomato juice. She will prepare spicy chicken wings to accompany our maize.

I know by now, because she always reverts to the wings; she prefers them over the carrots, beans, beetroots and cabbages she knows she should be eating. Dad said she could have any of the food he grows in the garden. Instead, she takes it home to her children: Lyness, and a boy whose name I do not know. She slaps her big African mama bum that I rest on when she ties me up in the blanket on her back, laughs, and says, "This is why you shouldn't eat my food." But still she lets me sneak

into her room, doesn't tell my dad that she feeds me most days. She should tell—in a way I wish she would, because then I won't be left at the kitchen table with a pile of vegetables still needing to be stuffed into my already-full tummy. If he catches me eating her food, I will be sure to feel his leather belt against the skin of my bottom. He tells me that it is his and Mom's duty to feed me, not hers; that it is not fair for me to eat her food. But I like hers more. I don't tell him this.

Finally, she takes her well-worn wooden spoon and stirs the now-stiff maize one last time. She scoops it high, and it slops down onto the plate into a perfect blob of white, delicious perfection. She makes her way down to her room at the bottom of the garden. She balances a metal tub of washing on her head, a tin plate with our steaming food in one hand, a tattered grass broom in the other. She sings all the while: a deep, low alto. I follow her, looking back to make sure Dad can't see me, to make sure he isn't watching through the kitchen window. I hope his study keeps him really busy for at least the next thirty minutes.

Together we settle into the cool dimness of her room. The light settles, my eyes start adjusting and pungent smells alternately waft to my nose: ash and soot, green Sunlight® soap, Vaseline® and acidic sweat that is my African mama. I'm looking for a fork, but there is none. She takes my little hand, shows me how to straighten my fingers, dig into the thicker-than-porridge mixture, then hold it in place with my thumb. I am fascinated by the warm sensation oozing through my fingers; I let out a childish squeal of delight. She "shooshes" me, tells me not to make Dad come looking for me. Next we dip the cooked maize into the spicy *chakalaka*, and she guides my hand to my mouth where I pop the mound into my cheeks. It is hot, and the steam escapes through my pursed lips as I joggle around the room, giggling, trying to cool down the lumps of hotness bouncing around in my mouth.

I look under the spring bed and see that it stands on bricks. I ask her why she wants a high bed. With cheeks full of pap and creviced lips smeared with sauce, she explains that the *tokoloshe* comes at night and if her bed is on bricks, he can't reach her. With my head tilted to one side, fingers breaking off chicken meat, I ask why that is. She says he is a short little man and can't reach up that high. I ask if he will steal her shoes that are lined up in a neat row under the bed.

She looks at me then, long and absorbedly, weighing her answer, wondering how much I can grasp. Her head shakes in a circular motion, and she says in a whisper that he is not interested in shoes, only bad people. This satisfies me, and my teeth keep working away at the sinew and cartilage, which will not loosen itself from the wing bone.

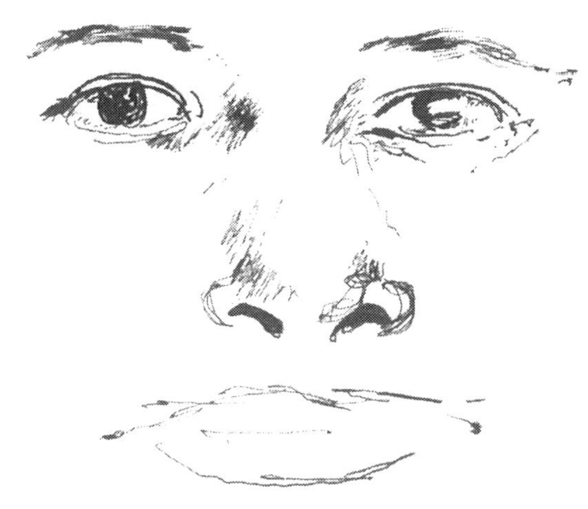

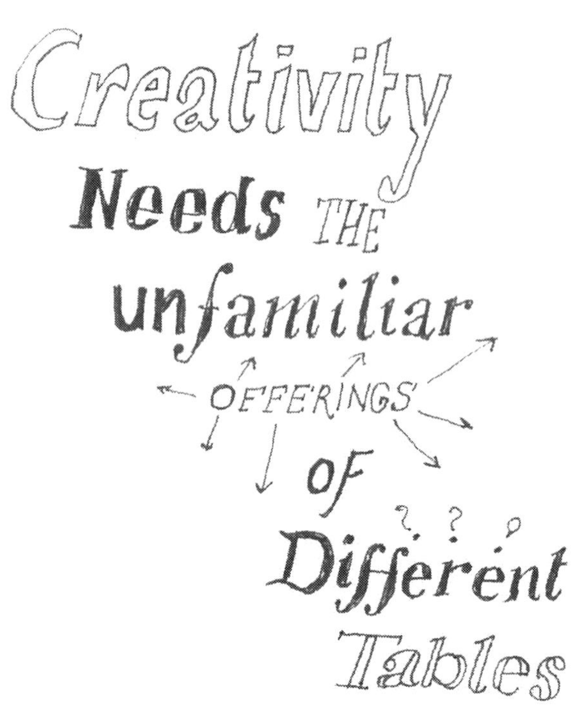

IN PURSUIT OF CREATIVITY:

1. WHAT IS UNFAMILIAR TO YOU THAT YOU LOVE DEARLY?
2. WRITE freely FOR 15 MINUTES ABOUT THE MOST unfamiliar experience that you have had. Describe the LIGHTING, THE SMELLS, THE objects, the feelings THAT SWELLED INSIDE of you.
3. Think carefully about unfamiliar SITUATIONS that have been shrouded in some kind of DIMNESS. What made them dim?

"i ask her why"

8 • The Midnight Owl

Creativity NEEDS the Surreal

"and then I am upside down and he is, too. i cannot wake from this dream"

I look up at her and see a ginormous fairy with a green, leafy skirt towering above me. She has a slender waistline: her bark forms a perfect corset, pulling her together in all the right places. Her leafy skirt is held in place by strong muscular branches that hoop outwards. She is the pride of our home; the pinnacle of the neighbourhood. Clearly visible above the red roof of the house, she is the reason many, many people call my daddy "friend." Of this I am sure. And it is the reason I come home from school every afternoon and have no problem staying out long after the sun has gone to bed. I imagine she feels restricted by the high wall that spans the yard directly behind her. The wall is covered with ivy, creating the perfect backdrop to a never-ending fairytale of made-up adventures in my ever-ripening mind. She is my very own avocado pear tree.

My mom doesn't know I climb to the branches that can barely hold me: balancing, testing, stepping out, balancing, testing, stepping out until one snaps and then I know I have reached the tender growth-point of my best friend. I sit down at that spot, wrap my skinny arms around her rough bark and hug her. I pat the underside of the branch, pretending it is a huge belly and I am riding on the back of a large unnamed creature that will take me to faraway lands where they make *chakalaka* and *pap,* just like my Margaret.

My daddy's friends come with their big boxes every July when the avocados are at their ripest: swollen wombs waiting to birth inner seed. The boxes are so big I can fit inside one, if I really try. If the friends don't have boxes, my daddy gives them his—the ones in which he packs books

he sells. The avocados are the length of a grown man's shoe. Daddy uses an extra-long swimming pool cleaning net that rests along the wall of the garage. We don't have a swimming pool, but we do have a very high avocado tree with fruit that needs picking every year. My 6'4" tall dad stands atop a five-rung wooden ladder at the base of the tree to steady himself. He swipes at the fruit with the net, attempting to loosen it from the knot that holds it to the branch. He tugs, tugs, tugs until it springs loose and lands in his net. His friends stand on guard, ready to catch the fruit if he misses it.

And so July passes. Friends come, friends go, friends come, friends go. Empty box. Full box. Bye-bye avocados. No problem, the tree bears more.

Towards the end of August, though, she tires of having her hair done with the pool net, rebels and stops producing those buttery, swollen wombs. The friends stop coming. The owls sense the putting away of the net and move in: a sign of early spring. The avocado tree will nest their two eggs, her long leafy branches providing a hideaway for their nighttime hunts and daylight watchtower duties.

My daddy decides they are his new friends. He sits in his wire garden chair, painted white and rusting from the soft loamy soil beneath, hooting at them, mimicking their cries. He explains to me that these owls have big, round, white, feathery faces. He talks deliberately with animated hands that absorb me into his world. He tells me their chests are spotted like the polka dot skirt I refuse to let Mom wash because then I can't wear it for a day. He says their noses are long and sloping like a banana covered in feathers with a sharp yellow beak at the end. I want to see one and Daddy says that only good girls get to see owls because owls hide from noisy children who climb into their trees. I wonder if I want to share my tree with these polka-dottish feathery creatures that have invaded my world. Mommy calls me in, bathes those terribly brown and mud-covered toes of mine, gets me pajama'd and into bed. I tell my dolls about the polka-dotted feather birds we need to hunt tomorrow. They tell me the snakes will catch me if I try to hunt the owls. They say little girls should never hunt owls. I drift fitfully as I always do. I fight sleep because it deprives me of mud cakes and avocado branches.

He rolls me over gently, whispering that I need to wake up quickly. I roll back over, imagining a dream. He whispers louder, more urgently. I am awake, pulling a doll along with me as my arms are herded into a night-gown. I am being picked up, my head landing limp on a shoulder that feels like Daddy's. "Come see the owls, Skruff."

"Which owls, Daddy? The polky-dotty feather ones?"

"Yes, those ones."

And then we are outside, under my avocado tree. The leaves are darker and hang like velveteen dresses on sticks. The stars sting the blackness. I am upside down now, hanging by my legs. I do not ask why this position is optimal. I assume polka dotty feather creatures need to see me differently than when I'm the right way up.

His white face is larger than any white feather face I have ever seen. He tilts his head upside down to mimic my upside-down one. Daddy turns me the right way up and polka dotty feather creature turns the right way up, too. And then I am upside down and he is, too. I cannot wake from this dream.

Daddy hoots at them and they talk back. All I hear is a long, shrill shriek. And then I am back in sleep land and being woken up for school. Was that really real?

IN PURSUIT OF CREATIVITY:

1. WHAT childhood experience was especially surreal and dreamlike in its unfolding to you?
2. Write in short bursts of SENTENCES FOR 15 MINUTES ABOUT SURREAL experiences that you recall from earlier years.
3. Think carefully about the mood that sets a surreal experience: WHAT LEADS UP TO IT, HOW LONG DOES IT LAST; DOES IT END AS IT STARTED?

CREATIVITY NEEDS THE SURREAL EXPERIENCE TO BROADEN THE Range of EMOTION

9 •

Creativity
NEEDS
COMPASSION

"i must know…so I can piece together why"

The bottom of the garden is like a haunted forest where a bedraggled witch resides. I imagine her hiding in one of the hibiscus trees. In this high-walled, thick-bushed area, all I hear from the other side is a lot of shouting and barking. Sometimes I am brave and weasel myself behind the sturdy branches. No one can see me here, especially if I have on the right-coloured clothes.

There is one place in the wall that the builders did not fill with enough cement, leaving a bubbled hole big enough for me to peep through and not get caught. I have a full view of the yard. It is surrounded by big trees: high ones that hang low, stooping towards the grass as if they are weighted down with burden. The grass is perfectly clipped, always. I can only see the back of the house: it is just a big whitewashed wall without shape or form. It simply rises high and ends, bluntly.

The voices are always there. One is their maid. I know that. I never see her, but her muttering in her native Sotho has become distinct. I have deciphered her incantations: high-pitched when angry, low in short bursts when annoyed. She's never happy; I never hear light-hearted singing or whistling. Another is the garden boy. I wonder why I never find him clipping the perfect lawn. Instead, all I hear are his large garden scissors clipping at an area I cannot see. Together, they mutter. Something is amiss over in this yard.

On other days, there is the shouting—consistently, all day long, about everything: the washing line, the wheelbarrow, the dog, the edge of the lawn, the flowers, the paving bricks, the shrubs. Everything. That voice belongs to a white man: an Afrikaans man who is cruel and does not like black people. These days are the days when I'm most afraid, even though it's just me and my cement-bubble-peep-hole.

I don't like his tone. I start memorizing the Sotho words. I must know what she complains about, so I can piece together why the other side of my wall is such an unhappy place.

When Margaret is busy with washing, I ask her what the words mean. She asks me where I heard them, and I tell her I heard her talking to her daughter. I think she knows I'm lying. I think she knows where I fetch these words.

Some days, especially after the rain, the bushes are too strangled for me to wrestle myself in. Instead I make mud cakes.

My swing set stands in the shade of the big avocado tree. My toes dig up the rich, loamy soil every day as I swing for hours arching my little hips skyward, hanging my head backward in an attempt to touch the leaves with my toes. I come down and as I push upwards, I fork up as much of that chocolate earth as I can. The smell of the damp soil intoxicates my little nostrils and the squishy earth oozing between my toes delights my senses. I know when the soil is just right. I slow myself down, bring the swing to a gentle swaying motion and jump off. I head straight for my watering can, dip it into the fishpond and carry it back to the unearthed mound I have created. I make this watering can trip ten times, with all the patience in the world. I am doing it for her. She is not muttering today, because she is hurting.

I take the rich soil into my little hands and mould it this way and that, looking at it from every angle to make sure it is just right. I pat, smack and pack. My head tilts to one side admiring my chocolate cakes all packed into the sun to bake. Stinker, the cat, comes strolling past, rubs against me with his hunched-up back. I whisper into his ear, telling him my secret.

I wait patiently as the chocolate cracks open in the sun. My cakes are ready. I dig around in my toy-box for the bowl with the pink edging. It will make her smile. I'm sure of that. I pack each chocolate cake carefully, making sure the edges don't break off. I carry it gingerly to the bottom of the garden, pushing it in under the bushes as far as I can. I wrangle myself in next.

I press my eye to my peephole. Her forehead is furrowed in downward lines. My little ears are blocked tight with my hands. The gruff man is screaming profanities: ugly words that Daddy has told me never ever to use.

I pick up my mud cakes, press my lips to the peephole and tell her about the chocolate I made for her. I tell her she mustn't listen to him. I tell her she is not that ugly word the man keeps calling her. I tell her I feel a deep-down kind of sad for her.

IN PURSUIT OF CREATIVITY:

1. WHAT SOCIAL ISSUES RILE you UP?
2. Allow yourself to be fully immersed into a social situation that you feel STRONGLY ABOUT. ALLOW THE FEELINGS THAT BOIL INSIDE OF YOU TO surface in your creative pursuits.
3. Create a character that exists within the SOCIAL DILEMMA YOU ARE ADDRESSING. CONTEXTUALISE THE CHARACTER WITH SOUNDS, SMELLS AND VISUALS.

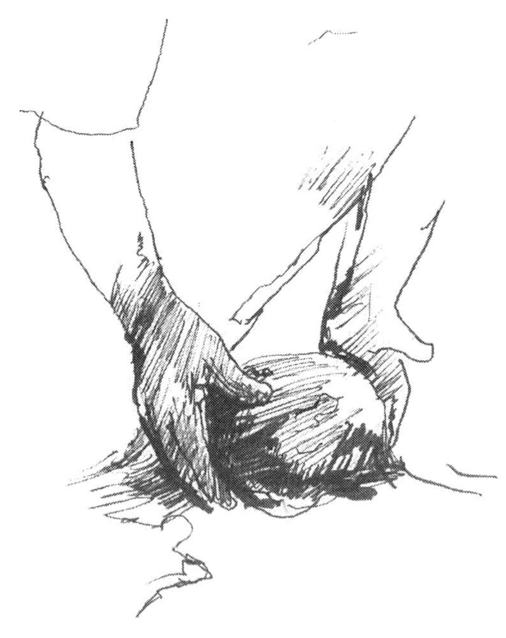

Creativity is fuelled by the anger brought about by INJUSTICE

9 lies I was told and believed

(ONLY FOR A WHILE)

ABOUT **CREATIVES**

• 10

1. CREATIVES ARE A SELECT GROUP OF PEOPLE IN THE HUMAN RACE

3. CREATIVES AREN'T GOOD LEADERS.

5. CREATIVES ARE PEOPLE WHO DRAW

6. CREATIVES CANNOT MAKE A LIVING WITH THEIR CREATIVE PURSUITS.

7. CREATIVE PEOPLE NEED A MUSE TO CREATE

8. Creatives ARE UN STABLE PEOPLE WHO ARE PRONE TO ADDICTION

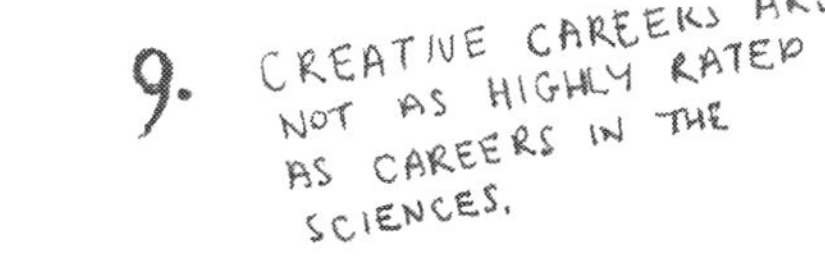

SCIENCE

11 •

creativity

needs

PEOPLE

"sometimes i have to look for them, but i always find them"

Slanted afternoon light floods the melamine kitchen floor, pooling around my legs and bouncing off my hair. The smell of cinnamon biscuits hangs thick in the air as Margaret removes another baking tray from the oven and tips it onto the tray waiting on the countertop. The biscuits will cool this evening and then tomorrow morning, early, she will pack them neatly into the tins Granny gave to Mom.

The world is as it should be: Mom is home from work sipping a cup of tea, absentmindedly staring out the window at the huge hibiscus blooms; I can hear Dad rustling around his office, finishing up his work day. Margaret neatly stacks the biscuits as she prepares to clean the kitchen before her day ends.

I reach up high but cannot quite get there. I stand on tippy toes and barely touch the side of the little black box. I rattle the cabinet until it moves closer to me. I grasp the box and pull it nearer until it loses balance and tilts forward into my little hands.

I find the "on" button and press it in deeply, waiting in expectation, and just like that, they are there: the voices, his and hers. And there is the tick-tock clock that always chimes when the hand of the big clock on the kitchen wall is at 12 and the other hand is at one of the other numbers that come after 12. Everything seems to be about the big number 12 on the clock. I wonder why it is such an important number. After the tick-tock clock there is always a different voice, and they read and read and read and read. I hear words like "Apartheid" and "Elections" and "Nelson Mandela." I have no idea what it is all about, but I listen.

I hold the box to my ear. I hold it up to the light, and I

notice that the light does not come through. It stops at the back of the box, causing a shadow to form on the floor. I tip it over and the voices go a little quieter. I tip it the right way up and the voices come back all loud and crispy clear. I hold it at a distance, both arms stretched out in front of me. I hold it to my ear like Dad does when he's watering the garden. I put it behind the door in the dining room and step back into the kitchen, listening intently.

My forehead creases up, my lips purse together and my eyebrows furrow as I think about this box. When I hear voices, I can see, always see, them. Sometimes I have to look for them, but I always find them. But these voices are different: they are inside the box. I walk through the house looking for them when Dad presses the "on" button, but I cannot find them. They also get softer, like when I tip the box over on its side.

I leave the box in its pool of light, lying on its side. I wonder if the people can feel it when I tip them over or turn them upside down. I see a place for a screwdriver on the back of the box, so I wander through the house, looking for the little tool box I got for Christmas. I need to find the voices. I want to see what she looks like. Does she have big blue eyes or deep dark brown ones? Does her hair curl or fall straight down her back? Does he have a beard, or is his skin bare and without prickly spikeys?

Mom calls down the passage, offering me a biscuit and a cup of milk. I run back with my screwdriver, telling her that she must wait for a bit.

Her puzzled face registers what my little hands are attempting, and she quickly swoops up the little black box. "Daddy will be very upset if you break his radio, Skruff."

"But I want to find the people."

IN Pursuit of CREATIVITY:

1. WHAT Type OF PEOPLE Do you FIND terribly INTERESTING?
2. Go TO A BUSY, PUBLIC SPACE. FIND A place to sit for a while. Settle in and note what keeps your attention: Is it the bizarre, the elegant or the RUN-OF-THE-MILL?
3. CAPTURE EITHER THROUGH SKETCHES, WORDS OR Images. WHAT THRILLS YOU about the characters passing BEFORE YOUR EYES?

12 •

CREATIVITY
NEEDS
FEAR

"i shake it, but it is locked. i shake it again"

My Tannie Irma had just been made boarding mistress for a prestigious girls' school in the northwest, and we all had to come visit to see her new home and classroom. Before even seeing it I could imagine the maps and the globe and the sand sediments. She so loved her geography. She was my favourite aunt, the one who picked on me least of all. She didn't call me names like the rest. She didn't treat me like a child. I liked her athletic calf muscles that stood firm and boldly on the back of her legs—testament to years of being a netball and hockey coach.

Our arrival is a whirlwind of darkness, suitcases being unpacked and hurried hellos from six aunts and uncles, all their husbands and wives and the many cousins in tow. After all the activity, my mom shuttles me into the bath, says I need to warm up before bedtime. She runs the water, fills it with bubbles and leaves the door slightly ajar so I can call if I need her. I hear her heels clicking down an endlessly long passage that seems to be taking her very far away from me. I hear my uncles laughing and swearing down at the far end of the house. I hear my aunts talking about food and the plans for the weekend. Food seems to be the centerpiece of every family weekend. I wonder why, because play seems far more important to me than eating. I lift my orange duck out of the water, nose-dive him back in, allow him to suck up a belly full of warm liquid, and then gun the bathroom down with water, pretending that my darling duck is a war machine. My sound effects drown out all noise from the far end of the house.

I keep gunning the mirror, filling my duck, spraying bubble bath until the water turns cold and my wrinkled skin starts irritating me. I don't like being 90 at four. I quiet down. Listen. Nothing.

I listen again. Still nothing.

"Mommy?"

Nothing.

There is not a sound in the house. All I hear are crickets having choir practice outside.

"Mooommmyyyy?"

Nothing.

I climb out of the bath, peep around the door to see if I can see someone.

No one.

I run down the passage, water dripping and the remainder of the bubble bath sticking to my bottom and the folds of skin under my arms. No one is in the house. I run all the way downstairs into the massive kitchen. Silence. Even the TV is muted.

Panic starts forming like a dough ball inside of my tummy. I can feel it fermenting and rising, choking me. Tears sting my eyes. Where is everybody and why did my mommy leave me in the bath? Where did they all go?

I run back into the bathroom, get back into the bath, fill my duck up, squirt his belly empty and listen. Nothing. I get out of the bath, run to the end of the passage, looking for someone, anyone, in any room. Nothing.

I find the front door after what seems like an eternity of running up and down the passage, shivering and slipping on tears. And I run as fast as my little legs can carry me to the gate. I shake it, but it is locked. I shake it again. And then I start screaming Mommy. Mooommmyyy. Moooommmmyyyyyy!

Nothing.

The wind comes up suddenly in a gust, and lightning fills the sky in bangs louder than gunshots. I run back into the house shaking and sobbing, coughing, spluttering. I climb back into the bath, stand there to warm my toes, jump out and run back to the gate with my orange duck.

I sob and inhale, trying to get air into my lungs that are so tight and sore. In that brief moment, I hear their voices. The wind carries the sound to me, but they are far away. I cry out again and again: Mommy!

And then she is there. Crying, sobbing. Saying sorry.

The sky doesn't look so dark anymore, but the house is a watery, soapy mess.

IN PURSUIT OF CREATIVITY:

1. When have you experienced absolute fear?
2. Think about the smells that you recall from this fearful experience. How do the smells differ from the smells on an ordinary day in your life? Describe the smells as specifically as possible.
3. Close your eyes and go through the moment of fear, sequence by sequence. Are some pants more blurred than others? How would you fill these in?

FEAR PROMPTS Creative SOLUTIONS EVEN IF THAT SOLUTION IS ONLY CALLING for HELP.

12 ways of capturing ideas on the GO → • 13

1. IN THE CAR (WHILE DRIVING): NO LEGAL SOLUTION FOUND JUST YET BUT VOICE NOTES INSIDE EVERNOTE WORKS VERY WELL

2. IN THE CAR (AS A PASSENGER): PHOTOS OF THINGS/PEOPLE/ PLACES THAT PROMPT IDEAS INSIDE EVERNOTE

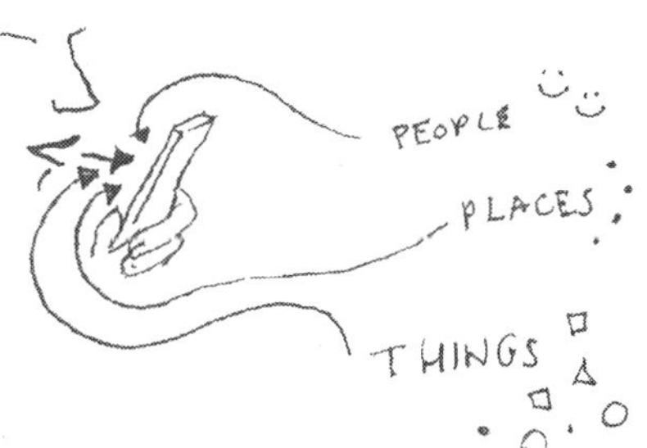

3. IN THE SHOWER OR BATH: BATH CRAYONS, PHOTO IN EVERNOTE AFTERWARDS

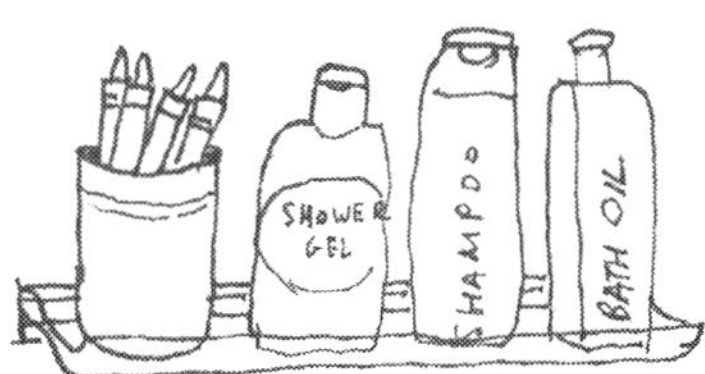

4. IN THE KITCHEN: PICTURE DRAWING IN THE SUGAR BOWL OR JOTTED DOWN ON THE SHOPPING LIST NOTEPAD

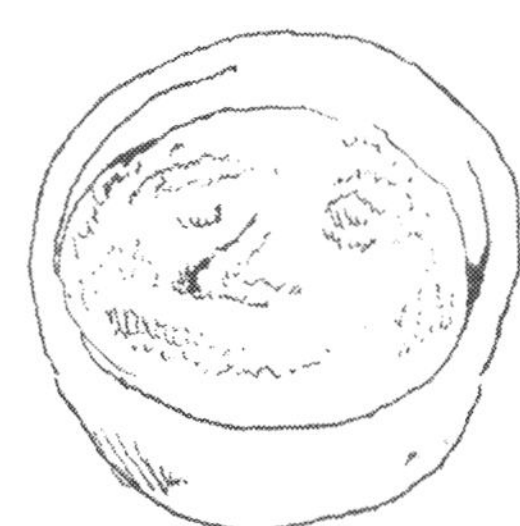

5. IN BED (IN THE MIDDLE OF THE NIGHT): IN THE JOURNAL THAT IS ALWAYS THERE, PHOTO IN EVERNOTE IN THE MORNING.

6. IN THE OFFICE (IF IT AFFECTS A DIRECTION I AM GOING IN): ON THE GOAL WALL.

7. IN THE OFFICE (IF IT IS SOMETHING THAT NEEDS TO BE MULLED OVER): IN MY JOURNAL.

8. IN THE OFFICE (IF IT REQUIRES ACTION ON MY PART TO PROGRESS IT): IN WUNDERLIST.

9. IN PUBLIC TRANSPORT: PHOTO IF POSSIBLE, POSSIBLY SNEAKILY IN EVERNOTE.

10. IN NATURE: BY TALKING TO THE PEOPLE WITH ME OR TO MYSELF (OUT LOUD, SHAKING MY HANDS AND HEAD).

11. WEEKENDS AWAY: IN MY JOURNAL

SAT SUN JOURNAL

12. ON MY MOUNTAIN BIKE: IT USUALLY ENDS UP IN THE MUD THAT I KEEP FALLING INTO. OOPS.

14 • Chasing Dust Motes

Creativity needs fascinated Experimenting

"i wonder if they have things inside their bodies that switch on"

The dining room is my favourite playroom. I am big and small all at once in this room. Small because just beyond the window is the long narrow garden that runs along the side of the house where the neighbour's cat hides, where poison ivy grows thick and wild, and where the roses tower towards the sun, which only slants in for brief periods of time. Big because there is something about the yellowwood dining room table—its smooth surface, its seemingly never-ending length—and the comfortable bench that runs along the wall, that entice me to make a house of the place.

I pretend to be the missus. My mom's far-too-large high heels clack on the floor as I walk about making shopping lists, checking my handbag and bossing the "children" around. At some point I decide that the rooms need to look roomier, and I lug most of the contents of my mother's linen cupboard down the passage and start erecting walls between the table's legs to make an even cosier home just under the table. I creep in, kicking the heels off on the way, and lie back, inhaling my secret space deeply.

I watch dust creatures drift through the light and linen. I hold my hands up, moving each finger first to the left, then to the right. I try to capture the creatures rather unsuccessfully, but the way my skin crinkles and uncreases itself distracts me. I sit upright, remembering that my skin feels different when I just get out of the bath. I wonder if I wash my hands and then try to catch the dust creatures, will they stick to my skin more successfully? I crawl out of my newly-built home and run to the bathroom. I let the tap run cold over my skin. I hurriedly flick my hands through the hand towel and race back to my position under the

table. I lie on my back, hands placed like a web in front of my eyes, searching, scrutinising the dust creatures and their landing positions.

My skin feels different all of a sudden: tighter, more elastic. The dust creatures aren't sticking as I'd hoped. I want my hands to be all soft and supple again. I push back out of my tented landscape and run to the bathroom. I try the warm water and smile at how my skin instantaneously feels different again. Towel, tent, dust creature stick-ability testing. So the afternoon ticks by, back and forth between tented-land and bathroom-water-source. My skin is drying faster and faster and losing hydration by the minute. I can't compute the physics or the chemistry, but my curiosity has me spellbound.

The sun dips below the wall, and the slant of light that made its way into my tent is gone. I pretend it isn't and keep moving my fingers wondering why the creatures are visible in the bright light but not in the shady light. I wonder if they have things inside their bodies that switch on when sunlight shines on them or if they are there all the time and sunlight just makes them come alive.

"Knock knock."

"Yes, Dad?"

"Can I come in?"

"Only if you take your shoes off at the door."

"My socks, too?"

"No, don't be silly. That would make my house stink."

"I don't think my feet stink!"

"They do. They smell like feet."

"What do feet smell like?"

"I don't know. But what do dust creatures smell like?"

"What are dust creatures?"

"Those things that switch on their bodies when the sun shines on them."

"Huh?"

"You know! If a room is full of sun then you see things dancing in the air? Those things."

"Oh, dust motes."

"Dust motes? Why are they called motes? Aren't motes the circle-rivers around castles?"

"Yes, moats are those things, too. Why are your hands so red?"

"'Cause I washed them 67 times today..."

"Why?"

"Well, you see, because I was trying to catch the dust creature mote things."

IN PURSUIT OF CREATIVITY:

1. What natural occurrences fascinated you as a child?
2. What aspect of nature fascinates you now and how you can go about finding out more about the physics or chemistry behind it?
3. THINK carefully about a naturally occurring event and document what you don't understand about it. Then ⟶ go away and find answers.

"Creativity NEEDS TO BE fascinated in the presence of the things it doesn't quite understand yet or maybe ever."

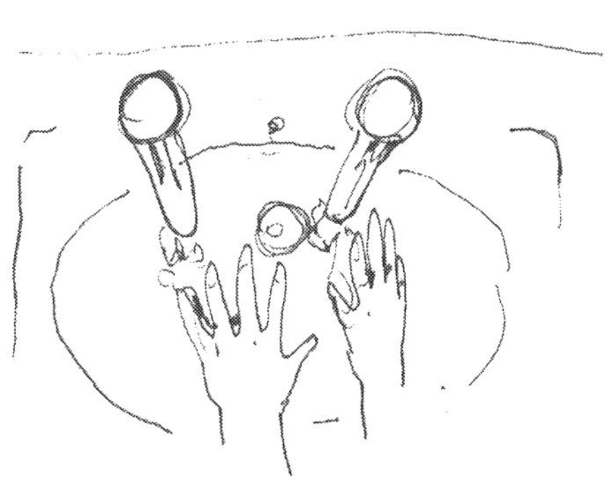

17 Lessons learned while writing this book • 15

1. SOMETIMES ANGRY MUSIC IS <u>GOOD</u>. #AMWRITING

2. MY TEENAGE SELF IS CAUSING GREAT IRRITATION IN ME. #AMWRITING

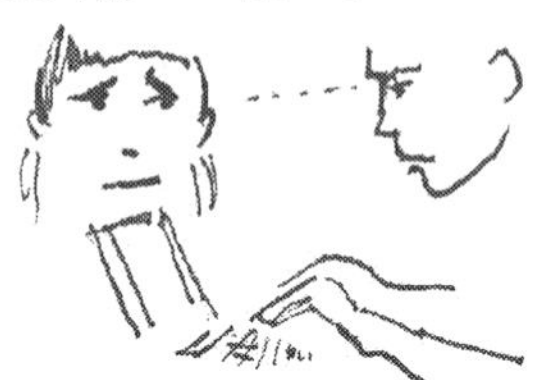

3. DIGGING FOR DETAILS... MEMORY FEELS JADED, WITHHOLDEN SOMEHOW. #AMWRITING

4. THE STORY WRITES ITSELF. #AMWRITING

5. WRITING DIFFERENT STORIES AT THE SAME TIME HAS ITS CHALLENGES. #AMWRITING

6. I AGREE WITH ANNIE DILLARD WHEN SHE SAYS 'IT MAKES SENSE TO WRITE ONE BOOK' RATHER THAN COLLECTIONS OF STORIES. #AMWRITING

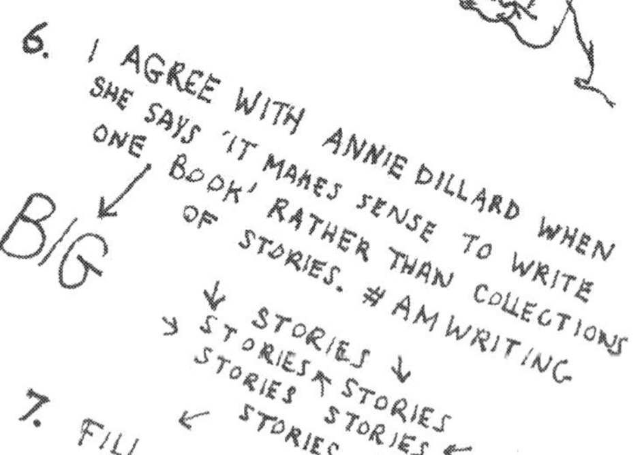

7. FILL IN THE ~~GAPS~~ DETAILS DON'T LET THE GAPS STOP THE STORY #AMWRITING

8. NEVER UNDERESTIMATE THE VALUE OF A PARENT IN THE WRITING PROCESS. THEY ARE A MINE. DIG. DIG. DIG. DIG DEEP. #AMWRITING

9. SOMETIMES I DISCOVER GOLD... AND THE STORY JUST UNRAVELS. #JUSTSAYIN' #AMWRITING

10. WRITING A BOOK IS A LOT LIKE HOW FRIENDS DESCRIBE GIVING BIRTH. #AMWRITING

11. IT'S EASY TO SKIM THE SURFACE. IT'S MORE REWARDING TO DIG DEEP

12. DESCRIBE A PLACE BY NOT DESCRIBING THE ACTUAL PLACE BUT RICH DETAILS WITHIN THAT SPACE. #AMWRITING

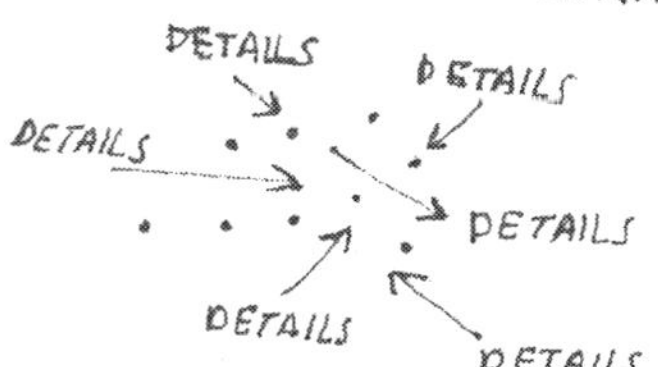

13. INDULGE MY SENSES PLEASE. #AMWRITING

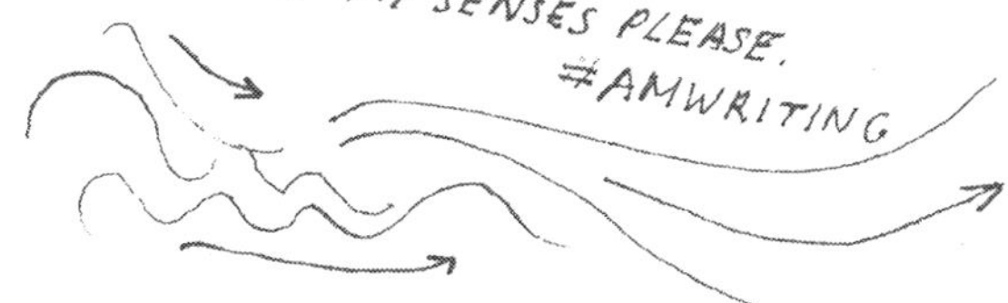

14. THE MUSIC YOU LISTEN TO WHEN WRITING INFLUENCES THE SUBTLETIES OF THE PIECE. #AMWRITING

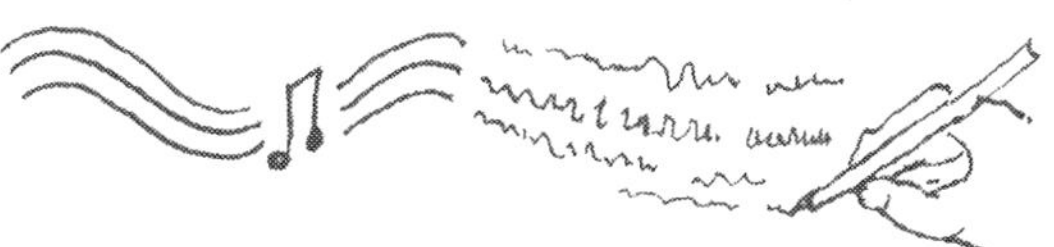

15. TURN OFF ALL DISTRACTIONS WHEN WRITING. #AMWRITING

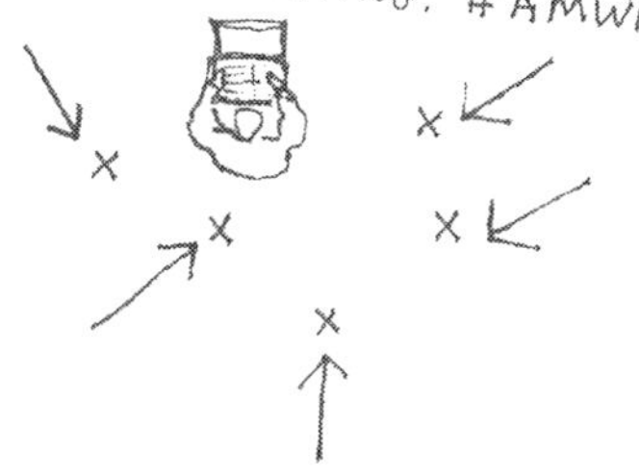

16. 7.30 AM – 9.30 AM WRITING WITH BREAKFAST AS A REWARD = WINNING RECIPE #AMWRITING

17. SUNSHINE ON MY BACK WHILST WRITING MAKES FOR SUNSHINE ON THE PAGE.

16 • Winning BUT losing

Creativity
NEEDS
to understand
Competition

"i knew what mattered to me. i knew what mattered to her"

Heat mirages ripple like oily steam in the distance. The heat pushes us, trying to find its way around our bodies. With no outlet, it runs down my armpits in perfectly formed sweat beads. The sky above is steel blue: the kind only Africa can produce consistently. Parents line the grassy banks of the track, hiding from the sun's scorch. Colourful umbrellas hide their eager, anticipatory faces as they search through the athletes to find their child. Trestle tables, big cast iron baths with ice and water, and that signature red-and-white tape form a horizon line in front of me. That is my goal: right there, up ahead.

We are at the bottom end of the grass track, away from the commotion that is ever-present on Athletics Day. The official motions with her hand, willing us into position. This is the final race. This is the one I need to win to make today one of complete victory.

I can hear Jane breathing next to me. She has it in her to beat me. I know that and I never underestimate her. Ever. She has fire in her belly. I close my eyes as we stand, minutes elongating into unrealistic time in my head. I can see her blue eyes, the way they pierce ahead. I can see her ink-black hair falling down her back, tied into a strangling ponytail. I am brought back, the cotton T-shirt clinging to my back discomforts me and I nudge my shoulders, pulling at the hem, allowing air to flow in.

"On your marks."

I hunker down and inward, but nobody knows this.

"Get set."

My legs rise but my heart restrains.

The gunshot ripples through the heat and so do I.

I sense her close behind. I forge forward. It all goes quiet, very quiet. I am chasing heat mirages ahead of me; chasing down the red-white tape that marks my victory. It is within reach, easy reach.

I stop short instead. The balls of my feet curve forward as I dig into the earth, stopping my white shirt from touching the tape. The red-white barrier ripples in the heat, still intact.

I turn; her ink-black hair grazes my cheek as her feet step over the white line and the ribbon streams out behind her hips as they forge powerfully around the track, finally coming to a stop.

Dad is next to me shouting, wondering why I stopped; teachers are confused, looking around trying to make decisions. She is walking towards me.

"Well done," I whisper.

This standing back, allowing another to break the ribbon happens multiple times. That day on the track was just the beginning. Many years later in a master's class, a professor explains McClelland's Need for Achievement (nAch) construct alongside the Need for Authority and Power (nPow) and the Need for Affiliation (nAffil). As he talks about characteristics that distinguish entrepreneurs and creatives, that day at the races comes flooding back to me along with every conversation where I have been labelled as competitive.

Inwardly I know myself not to be competitive, but my limited vocabulary prevents me from phrasing it differently. I have simply allowed the juxtaposition to exist inside of me.

The need for achievement: the challenge of the achievement itself is more important than the outcome. To others, the outcome matters. I knew what mattered to me. I knew what mattered to her.

IN Pursuit of CREATIVITY:

1. WHAT COMPETITIVE situations have you been in, that have been difficult to navigate?
2. What is more important to you: the outcome or the process?
3. LIST out competitive situations that you are currently dealing with. Make note of what is more important to the person you are in competition with.

"Competition either propels or stifles creativity. KNOW THE DIFFERENCE AND WHERE TO FIND THE PROPELLING TYPE."

17 •

Creativity Needs Ritual

"this is friday night"

Mom and Dad leave work early, and we try to get out of the city before it becomes crammed full of cars and trucks and people all pushing, inching, nudging forward, wanting to get someplace out: anywhere away from city-center-African madness. The road snakes north. In my mind I have created landmarks for myself that mark distance: the first toll road with the sky restaurant that runs over the highway like a bridge, the place next to the road where the shanty town shacks start, the white cross with someone's name on it, the vineyards, the big water tower.

We turn the corner. I count the houses from there until we turn into the driveway. Granny times it so she does not miss our arrival. She is fidgeting with her rose bush. At the sight of our car she looks up and smiles. I am out of the seat buckles and running barefoot into her arms, plunging my head into the folds of her skirt.

Chatter settles into calm as crickets and frogs start chorusing for the night. The smell of jasmine is thick in the air. The end of the week lingers in our midst as we take our seats at the round, heavy yellow-wood table. The chairs are covered in soft black leather that envelops the body when you sink into them. Supper is served generously: always too much.

After supper she clears the dishes and I can hear the little pot clattering as it makes its way from the cupboard to the stovetop. I hear her open the fridge and lift out the large bucket of milk that is delivered fresh daily from a nearby farm. The milk makes its way down the side of the enamel pot and then silence follows. It persists until a slight change in temperature occurs and the warped little pot starts a kind of dance on the stove top, mimicking my five-year-old impatience in the dining room next door: a sort of bobbing up and down from one bum cheek to

the next. The bubbles start forming, and a creamy layer of milk skin indicates this beautiful white stuff is almost ready to become cocoa.

She always taps the tin of cocoa. I can hear it, and that means warm cocoa is a few short minutes away from being inside my tummy. I hear the little pot touching the side of the ceramic cup she pours it into; I hear the tin being opened and the quiet means the cocoa is being measured out in her always-present precision. The slight beating sound: spoon whirring against ceramic side means that she will be appearing through the doorway any minute now.

And there she is, my cocoa in hand.

I grasp the cup with my little hands, feet dangling beneath the table, stroking the cat while I am at it.

This is Friday night.

"she always taps the tin of cocoa"

IN Pursuit of CREATIVITY:

1. WHAT family traditions have you carried over from childhood into your adult life?
2. WHAT TRADITIONS have you forgotten about that MEANT SOMETHING to you?
3. Introduce a simple ritual into your life and invite friends or family to share in it.

"Creativity blooms WITHIN MEANINGFUL repetition of daily habits."

9 disciplines that make the *process* of CREATION happen effortlessly

• 18

1. SHOWING UP TO CREATE, REGULARLY

2. WRITING DOWN EVERYTHING THAT I FEEL ABOUT EVERYTHING ON MY MIND, BEFORE I START CREATING

EVERY THING

3. CARVING TIME INTO MY WEEKLY SCHEDULE TO CREATE

MON	TUE	WED	CREATIVITY	THURS	FRI

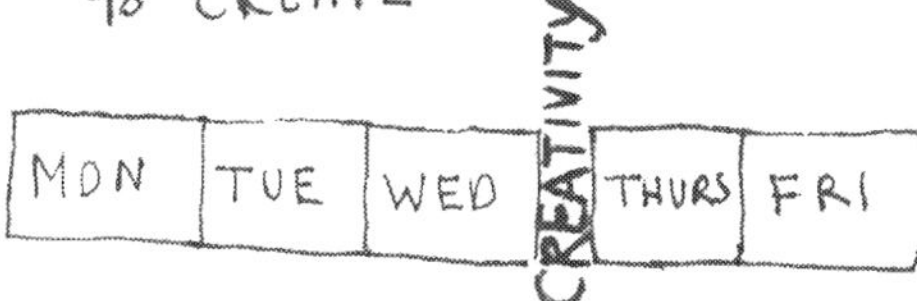

4. TAKING MY SELF ON ARTIST DATES

5. INVITING OTHERS TO JOIN MY ARTIST DATES SOMETIMES

6. DEVELOPING MY TASTE BUDS

7. DEVELOPING MY APPRECIATION FOR SOUND

8. LIMITING MY EXPOSURE TO ACTIVITIES THAT DEMAND OF ME TO BE A CONSUMER IN MY THINKING AND DOING.

9. KNOCKING ON STRANGERS' DOORS AND ASKING TO HAVE A CUP OF TEA

19 •

Creativity

needs

the

edge

"i am up on the bike, flying down the drive, through the air, over the edge and into the mess again, and again, and again"

Inching forward, I straddle the too-large bike seat. My legs and arms are bare; my dripping hair hangs down my back, making me feel cold. I'm only wearing a little pink bikini. The sun was too hot in the water, so I decided to occupy myself on the bike under the trees for a while. My knee and elbow guards, along with my helmet, lie forgotten in my bedroom.

I shouldn't be on this bike, but my generous father gave away my own bicycle to some ex-convict who needed a fresh start in his post-time life. I arrived home from school to witness the end of the transaction. At the age of nine, I was painfully aware that this was not going to be an easy parting.

I need to learn how to cycle this too-large bike, which is challenging when your house is built on a nearly perpendicular hill with a driveway so long and curvy it takes a car a good five minutes to reach the top.

I am braking myself from flying forward by straining hard on my calves. I started this at the top of the stone driveway that ends in front of our double-door garage. The driveway curves sharply to the right because straight ahead there is a sheer drop-off the length of a door, just past the mulberry tree. To the left of the mulberry tree on the edge of the drop-off is the four-row, bricked rhubarb garden and just below the edge is the compost heap: sweaty and emulsive in its rotten state. The smell is earthy and suffocating in the sweltering summer heat.

My plan is to sit properly in the saddle once I've cleared the turn in front of the tree and compost heap drop-off. This gives me a relatively long run of at least another ten metres before a disastrous cactus garden waits with all its poison and prickliness. I plan to get used to the new handle bars and pedals on this ten-metre stretch before having to focus really hard to clear the cactus garden and come back up again with every ounce of might that my little legs can muster against those big wheels. I reckon my plan is well-thought-out and execution will run seamlessly.

I stop inching forward and let myself go: I fly down the first few metres just as I expected I would. I start turning the bike to avoid the drop-off. All continues according to plan until I push lightly on the brakes to ease into the corner. I push a little harder, not feeling anything in the wheels. Another push—still nothing. I push down all the way but feel nothing. The bike is picking up speed by the second, and I realise I do not know this large frame well enough to avoid the cactus garden or the heavily-trafficked road waiting at the bottom of the driveway. My little mind is darting in front of my eyes as if I am watching myself in a cartoon during breakfast. The brakes are not working. I press, press, press, press—hoping—but nothing. I have no choice but to fly straight over the edge. I know the stinky compost is below, but right now that is the least of my worries. Before the edge I need to clear low-hanging mulberry branches that are hard and strong. They gnarl like an old woman's hands that have cooked and cleaned for too many children for too long. The crossbar of the bike is solid and straight: I am on my dad's bicycle, so I can't slide into the section that normally slopes down for ladies. I can't swing my leg over and abandon the bike because the frame is too big for me. I can't let my hands go because I will lose balance and fall on the hard brick drive, which will hurt far more than landing in compost.

At the very last second I just look straight ahead and fly.

The rhubarb streaks past me. I feel the big, granular leaves scraping my skin. A mulberry whips against my cheek and forehead and I feel its ripe juice running down over my eyebrows. I must have been crying unawares, because my mouth fills with a delicious taste of rich, salty berry juice at about the same time that I land softly into the middle of the vilest of smells. I lie in the warmth of the mushy mess, peeping at the cars through the cactus garden. Laughter rolls out of me like a chameleon tongue.

I am up on the bike, flying down the drive, through the air, over the edge and into the mess again, and again, and again.

Mom makes sure that I scrub up good that night.

IN Pursuit of CREATIVITY:

1. WHEN have the brakes FIGURATIVELY FAILED you with surprising consequences?
2. Plan an adventure which INVOLVES AN element of DANGER, AN object that you really LOVE AND an activity that really S T R E T C H E S you.
3. Record the process with a voice note after you HAVE completed the exercise. Describe in detail the feelings you had.

Creativity
NEEDS TO ride
OFF OF THE
edge
EVERY NOW
and then.

Sugaryard

Creativity
needs
to have
a market

"they all stream past, balancing paper cups and crumbs in already-empty plates"

Trays, trays, trays. And then more trays.

I am balancing one precariously on my little grey school-uniformed lap. Dad is holding one with his hand behind the seat, manoeuvring the steering wheel with his free hand. The rest of the shiny metal platters are hanging on for dear life as Dad makes his way through traffic, huffing, puffing and bemoaning every slow motorist around us. We need to get there quickly. My foot taps incessantly against the plastic gearbox. Dad swats my leg. A ceramic bee flies off the edge of the tray and falls. My first inventory item has broken and I haven't even opened shop yet!

The sun is baking in through the windscreen. I can feel the heat against my neck, sticking there, making my school shirt an uncomfortable fit. My eyes move across the backs of each and every wing, every striped body that I meticulously painted with painstaking nine-year-old accuracy. I hope my customers don't notice the occasional streaks and blotches.

Our car screeches into the dusty parking lot. Dad shoves two trays under his arms, blusters out the door, and marches into the building. I try to keep up, but my substantially-shorter legs can't keep pace with his six-foot frame. I give up and admire my ceramic magnet creations one more time. I smile. I love them dearly. This is their moment to shine. For a few weeks now I have been working on them in my little factory down the stairwell that leads to the basement. Mrs Appleby made such a big fuss over this Entrepreneurship Day, you'd think we were starting the next big business to take over the world. Maybe we are. That is, if sugar plans to take over the world.

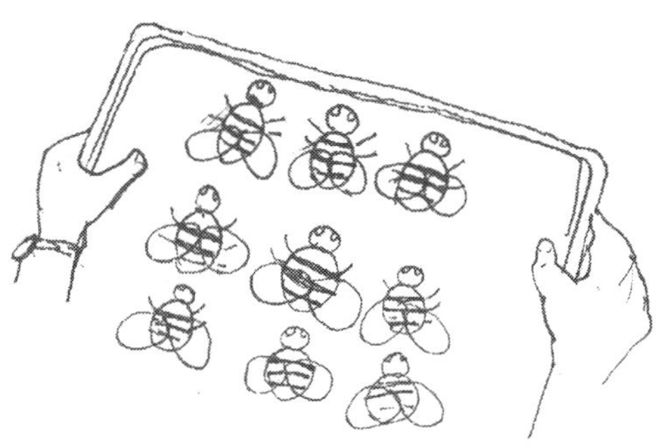

I turn the corner, climb the two oversized steps and enter the courtyard. Sunshine skirts around trestle tables, beating down hard on anything and everything. Teachers and parents scurry this way and that with umbrellas to protect child-skin and chocolate cakes, chocolate cupcakes, chocolate-covered biscuits, chocolate ice cream, chocolate milkshakes, chocolate suckers, chocolate drinks. I stand back wondering if anyone made anything for this day apart from chocolate-somethings. Willy Wonka would be proud.

I walk to the spot under the library stairs where Dad found an empty table on which he hurriedly placed my trays and trays of winged plaster cast creatures before leaving with a "see you later." My next-door neighbour is clad in an apron with chocolate streaks down the front. She's wearing a baker's cap, which has slid slightly down the left-hand side of her blond hair. She smiles and waves as she sets out the big cake knife alongside the plates and her change jar.

We head inside for the blur of morning lessons. We keep peeking sideways out the windows with aching eyes and bellies at all the tables. Entrepreneurship Day is half-class day. We all fidget, waiting for eleven bells to chime in the church clock down the road. The buzzer will sound shortly after that, at which point all forms of coordinated mayhem will descend as little mouths and their parents scurry around the courtyard admiring the creations.

My bees look even better in the direct sun. The yellow and black patterns gleam. I take position behind my table and wait eagerly for money to start rolling in. I've calculated my possible profits. I know my expenses. I owe nothing because I loaned from my own savings, but I would like to replenish that because I really want to buy myself a new bedroom suite in the next two years. My change is neatly packed into a plastic container under the table.

Sally and her mom walk past and ask me how I made the bees. They do not buy. Shaun's dad stops to touch the wings, doesn't look at me until I say a timid "Hello oom." He nods and buys a slice of cake from next door. I am not worried. The day has only just started and people are milling everywhere. I smile, greet and explain how I moulded each little creature, dried it, painted it and fixed the magnets to the back.

Natalie, Janice, Heleen, Myra, Minke, Candice, Chantelle: they all stream past balancing paper cups and crumbs in already-empty plates.

I glance up. The courtyard is emptying out. A plastic cup blows across the cement and gets stuck under the gutter. I hear clinking change-jars as my friends count their day's takings. Empty cake containers are closed up, placed into baskets. Serviettes are used to clean off knives.

I glance down. I made one sale all day. My change container looks like it did that morning. My bees are no longer in the sun as the imposing staircase casts a looming shadow over them. They don't look so pretty anymore.

Dad can't pick me up. I have to take the bus home. I ask Mrs Appleby if I can store all the trays in the back of the class until a day when Dad can pick them up for me. They stare at me for three weeks after that, especially in math class when I try to do multiplication.

I slide all my carefully-packed bees into a large plastic bag. I hear wings chipping as they hit each other on the way to the bottom. At home, I stuff them into the back of the pink cupboard that makes up my little factory. I don't go back there for seven weeks. I play in the vine branches where I swing back and forth, trying to work out why I decided to make and tried to sell bees when all everyone wanted was sugar.

"Creativity
is
as much
about
MARKET
KNOWLEDGE
as
IT IS
ABOUT
Creation"

IN Pursuit of CREATIVITY:

1. When you share your creations, what really gets a response?
2. HOW does your audience respond and what do these responses say about your audience?
3. MAKE a list of things that your audience has really responded to when you have shared them.

My 5 earliest Creative ~~Mistakes~~ • 21

~~(all made between~~
(all learned in second grade):

~~1.~~ Making stuff my market didn't want then having to deal with unwanted inventory after entrepreneurship day at school.

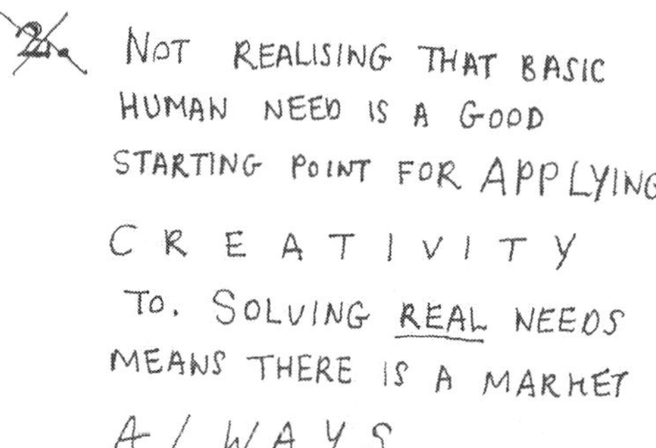

~~2.~~ Not realising that basic human need is a good starting point for applying creativity to. Solving REAL needs means there is a market always.

~~3.~~ Creating for my own pleasure and assuming my potential market would want what I liked and made for myself.

~~4.~~ Creating craft items and selling it in a schoolyard when art of this nature would be more fully appreciated in another environment.

CREATING by not Copying

Creating by NOT COPYING

~~5.~~ 6. Not asking all the other vendors at entrepreneurship day what they would be selling.

22 • Tables and tunnels

Creativity

NEEDS

A

⟶ change of Environment

"i like my dining room tables to change"

I am visiting 95 Blackwood Street again today. Clifford and I are on a Famous Five mission; the only difference is that we are two and not so famous. We're digging tunnels beneath the floor of his house. We sneak through the trapdoors when Matthew goes to the bathroom. Our headlamps show us the next patch of bricks we need to sweep up to rid the place of cobwebs and copious amounts of dust. The primary aim of all this darkened domesticity is an elaborate attempt to get rid of pestering little brothers who disturb our playtime and make lots of noise when they really should be quiet.

Matthew hears the broom knocking against the wooden floorboards and starts calling for us. We go dead quiet, wait for him to leave before we resume our serious work. We have a tunnel to dig: who knows where it might lead?

Our grumbling tummies and dust-tickled noses pull us up out of the tunnel's interconnected passageways and into the kitchen where a big pot of red spaghetti awaits us: my personal favourite and also the reason I keep threatening to pack my bags and leave home. We don't eat red spaghetti at my house, you see.

We wolf down the gluten-sticky threads, wipe tomatoed mouths and start planning how to get Matthew distracted again.

This weekly eating of red spaghetti, tunnelling and Matthew-ridding is a constant I escape to. Clifford's house has a homey feel to it. Things match and furniture doesn't change. The weekly menu is pretty constant. Back home on my terrain, things are a little less constant.

Dad has this compulsive habit of giving things away. He believes we have more than enough of everything and some others don't. He talks earnestly to me about this matter on a regular basis and encourages me to share wherever I can. The reality sank in when I was about seven and arriving home from school one afternoon.

~

The school bus drops me off at the gate and I start the long walk up the winding driveway that leads to our house nestled among the trees, high up on the hill. I've hooked my thumbs through my satchel straps and I'm paying close attention to ants scurrying around my feet when out of nowhere, my bicycle rolls towards me with some odd man riding. He looks rough, with messy hair, pock-marked skin, and stubble starting high on his cheeks and travelling all the way down to his navel, which I can see through missing buttonholes. His pants are ironed, but dirt is pressed into them. I stop dead in my tracks, staring after my bicycle disappearing down the driveway. I would chase had I not seen Dad standing at the open garage door, waving the man on his merry way.

My thumbs unhook from their comfortable satchel position, motioning upwards, sideways, looking for explanations. He pulls me in tight as I near him.

"When he is bringing my bike back, Dad?"

"He isn't. He needed transport."

"Will my bike take him far?"

"Farther than his feet."

"Oh, ok. Will you buy me another bike?"

"One day, when I have money again."

I am able to put his words into practice in smaller ways. I share my lunchbox at school. I give my toys away. But the bigger items in my life remain a struggle. It's not only a struggle for me—Mom also wonders where things disappear to. I remember the dining-room-table-day very clearly.

I arrive home but can hardly get into my own gate, let alone reach the front door. A rusty trailer is parked at an odd angle, and the yard is bustling with men. Oak chairs and a huge dining room table stand scattered like chess pieces across the yard. I try to make it to the door but get hauled into a line of people who carry the table into its new home: my home.

"Where's my dad?" I ask no one in particular.

"He's helping Anthony set up his flat."

"Who's Anthony?"

"Dunno. I do know he just got here from Zimbabwe."

"Right. Did he take anything with him when he left here?"

"Yes. Your dining room table."

"The round yellowwood one?"

"Yes, it was round."

I walk into the house shaking my head. Mom will be surprised in all the wrong ways tonight. She loved that table. I wonder if Dad remembered to give away the round tablecloths that don't fit on any other table for Anthony's new flat, too.

There are fireworks that night. I hide behind my math textbook, but long division offers little solace. It doesn't make sense, either.

Mom wants her table back. Dad says he thinks the new one he found at an auction will be just fine for us. Anthony's apartment is oddly shaped and the circular shape works better than a rectangular one.

~

These memories run around in my mind every time I go back to 95 Blackwood Street where the paintings stay fixed on the same wall, the couches get indentations from being sat on in the same way, and the table gets more scarred and marked from each family meal.

We are tunnelling again today. This time Matthew isn't fooled. He is tunnelling with us and kicking up way too much dust for our liking. This is our space, and we don't want dust. We take a break to gobble down all the glorious red spaghetti. We're planning to head back into the tunnel to read the next chapter in the Famous Five book series. We're also planning to find a way out of the tunnel into the garden.

We give Matthew permission to join this adventure. Just this once.

The house might be cosy, the menu constant, but there is a reason I keep going back to the tunnels. I like my dining room tables to change.

IN PURSUIT OF CREATIVITY:

1. When have you resisted change?
2. What can you do today to tunnel into a new area you really want to discover?
3. Make a list of things you want to do but that scare you too much to attempt. Choose one and then brainstorm ten things you can do that will move you in that direction or, at the very least, help you to take the next step.

"CREATIVITY *thrives* ON CONTINUAL *change* WHILST SIMULTANEOUSLY *resisting it.*"

23 • NOT A MORNING Person

Creativity
NEEDs
to know
itself

"good walls make good neighbours"

Annette Banda. That's what she is called, but I think her mom made a mistake. She should've called her Tracey Chapman, junior. Her voice is as deep and melodic, her shoulders as broad and her skin as chocolate.

Annette writes good stories. She writes such good stories that Mrs Botha asks her to read them aloud to the class. Today is no different. Her voice starts in that low alto but I get stuck at sentence one. She describes her breakfast bowl and its milky content as an island with little mountain peaks puffing out all over the place. I am smitten and instantaneously transported to a world that makes such a strong impression on me that every morning after that, over my own bowl of cereal, I see Annette's face, hear that voice and imagine the good island life.

Morning time is not my happy time. I like sleep, and I don't like the dark. Alarms make me grumpy. Dad, on the other hand, gets so excited about mornings, he wakes up at 4:00 a.m., chirping this beautiful hour of the day away as I mentally block out all sounds.

Family breakfast at our household is an affair fit for a queen and her household. The white tablecloth is laid. Each person's place is set out to perfection with folded cloth napkins in serviette rings. An extravagant platter of fruit is prepared using four or five different in-season fruits at their ripest. Toast, muffins, fresh bread, chilled fruit juice, tea, coffee, honey, peach jam, strawberry jam, apricot jam, raspberry jam, marmalade, Marmite®—an assortment of condiments so varied they assume more than half of the table space.

This is centre stage. I want to eat my bowl of cereal in silence while being transported to that sun and white sand that Annette captured perfectly for me. Dad wants to talk about the day ahead, the sound of

the birds, his plants, whatever he read that morning—anything, really. I grunt replies, hoping he will understand my need for silence. This request delivered via eye rolling and a teenaged stare is met with every reason why morning truly is the most magnificent time of day. I try to sink further into my supposed island life, conjuring up mental images of pushing my head into the milk and soggy cereal, my hair fanned out around me. I wonder if resorting to that extreme would keep him quiet.

Eventually the war rages long enough and my morning sensibilities reach their limit. I start building a wall. Interestingly, Mrs Botha has been discussing Frost's "Mending Wall" with us. I find it appropriate to start mending this wall between Dad and me by building it in the first place. The jam jars are my bricks.

I simply line them up on the piece of tablecloth between the bowls and cutlery that separates my "yard" from Dad's "yard." He notices but doesn't say anything.

Day 2: I reconstruct the same wall. He puts his banana peel on my side of the wall after chopping the fruit into his island-life-cereal-bowl. I remove it and place it on his side of the wall.

Day 3: I construct a second wall in front of me from the cereal boxes that usually live at the upper end of the table. The first wall between us goes up as well. He does nothing.

Day 4: I construct three walls, all around me, from cereal boxes, jam jars and milk bottles. He places his coffee cup inside my wall. I remove it, saying, "Good walls make good neighbours." His lip protrudes as it always does when he is thinking. "Interesting," he states.

Day 5: I construct three walls. He knocks on a jar. I stare into my island life. He leaves.

Day 6: I construct three walls. He constructs three walls using the cereal boxes. I say nothing.

Day 7: He constructs three cereal box walls first. I construct three jam jar walls. We eat our island-lives in silence. I peep over the boxes. He ignores. He sits up straighter and peers at me over the top of the boxes: “Curiosity killed the cat, you know.”

And so the morning conversation starts. We both know who wins this war.

IN Pursuit of CREATIVITY:

1. What natural rhythms do you want to take into account when being creative?
2. Keep a diary for a week:

   Listing what your natural inclinations are. When are you most tired? When are you more energised? When do you need silence? When do you need company?
3. Create a weekly blueprint for yourself in which you break down the days of the week into time slots. Schedule creative activities around optimal times.

A weekly BLUEPRINT (AND why YOU need ONE)

• 24

A WEEKLY BLUEPRINT ALLOWS YOU TO STRUCTURE YOUR WEEK SO THAT YOU ARE ACTIVELY MAKING TIME FOR CREATIVITY. YOU GET MORE DONE THIS WAY. I CALL IT INCREMENTAL PROGRESS.

A GOOD WAY TO APPROACH YOUR BLUEPRINT IS AS FOLLOWS:

1. THINK ABOUT ALL THE AREAS THAT MAKE UP YOUR DAILY LIFE. IT IS IMPORTANT TO INCLUDE ALL ASPECTS THAT HELP US TO BE WHOLE BEINGS BECAUSE IT IS IN EACH OF THESE AREAS THAT WE DISCOVER OUR CREATIVE SELVES. TYPICAL CATEGORIES COULD INCLUDE:

   a. Marriage/Partnership
   b. Spiritual
   c. Business
   d. Learning
   e. Physical
   f. Relational
   g. Cultural/Travel
   h. Sleep

2. LOOK AT YOUR WEEKLY BLUEPRINT AND CONSIDER HOW YOU CAN SLOT TIME INTO YOUR DAILY LIFE TO ENSURE THAT YOU ARE BECOMING A MORE "WHOLE", CREATIVE PERSON WITH EACH PASSING DAY.

3. REMEMBER THAT YOUR WORK CAN BECOME AN OUTLET FOR CREATIVITY IF YOU CHOOSE TO VIEW IT IN THIS WAY AND ACT ACCORDINGLY.

4. BE INTENTIONAL ABOUT SLOTTING CREATIVE TIME AROUND FIXED SCHEDULES THAT INCLUDE WORK AND CHILDREN.

5. REMEMBER TO SLOT IN ENOUGH SLEEPING TIME FOR YOURSELF.

I CAN FUNCTION WELL ON 7 HOURS OF SLEEP. YOU MIGHT NEED 10.

my blueprint

TIME	MONDAY	TUESDAY	WEDNESDAY	THURSDAY	FRIDAY	SUNDAY
06.00	QUIET TIME	QUIET TIME	QUIET TIME	QUIET TIME	QUIET TIME	
07.00						
08.00			SWIMMING	SWIMMING	ADMIN	
09.00	ADMIN	ADMIN		SWIMMING	PHOTOGRAPHY	GARDENING
10.00	CLIENT WORK	CLIENT WORK			CODING	MEAL PLANNING
11.00			Client Work	CLIENT WRITING	READING	COOKING
12.00			Client Work	CLIENT WORK	BUDGET	WASHING
13.00						WEEKLY PLANNING
14.00	SALES	SALES				
15.00				NEW BOOKS		
16.00						
17.00			Client Work			
18.00		DATE NIGHT	CULTURE NIGHT/OPEN			
19.00			PERSONAL WRITING			PERSONAL WRITING
20.00	EXERCISE			EXERCISE		
21.00						
22.00						
23.00	SLEEP	SLEEP	SLEEP	SLEEP	SLEEP	

create your own blueprint

TIME		MONDAY	TUESDAY	WEDNESDAY	THURSDAY	FRIDAY	SUNDAY
06.00							
07.00							
08.00							
09.00							
10.00							
11.00							
12.00							
13.00							
14.00							
15.00							
16.00							
17.00							
18.00							
19.00							
20.00							
21.00							
22.00							
23.00							

NOW, WHAT TO DO WITH THIS 

Keep it with you in a diary

Stick it up on the wall where you can see it every day

put one on the fridge

TELL YOUR FAMILY ABOUT IT

PLAN YOUR WORKDAY AROUND IT

MONDAY 1

KEEP...... 12:00
TO 12:07
ALLOTTED . 12:09
TIMES...... 12:21

CHANGE IT REGULARLY
AS YOUR SCHEDULE CHANGES

CUT BACK ON ACTIVITIES THAT ARE NOT CONTRIBUTING POSITIVELY.

+1 START WITH ONE CREATIVE ACTIVITY PER WEEK.

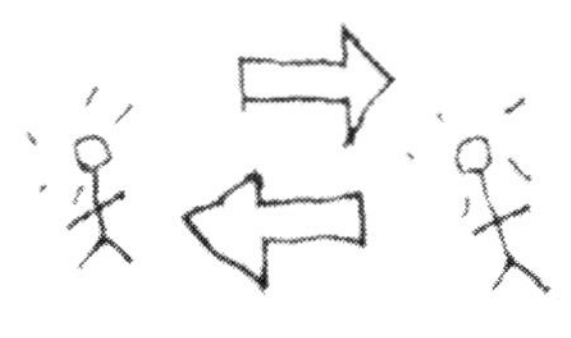

ASK A FRIEND TO BE YOUR ACCOUNTABILITY PARTNER AND SHARE IT WITH HIM OR HER

FIND A CREATIVITY PARTNER

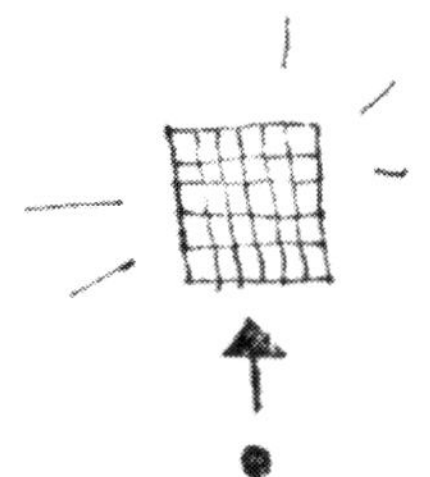

GET YOUR CREATIVITY PARTNER TO CREATE A WEEKLY BLUEPRINT, TOO.

A MASTER LIST • 25

(AND WHY YOU NEED ONE OF THOSE TOO)

CREATE A LIST AND CALL IT YOUR MASTER LIST.

THIS LIST NEEDS TO BE IN A PLACE THAT YOU CAN ACCESS AT ALL TIMES.

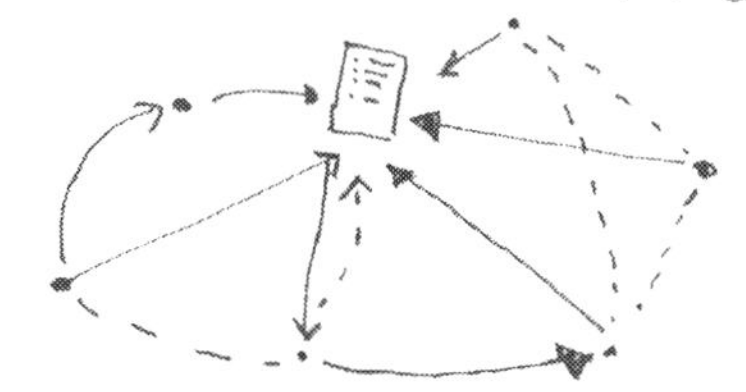

I RECOMMEND A MOBILE PHONE, USING A LIST APP SUCH AS any.do or Wunderlist.

THINK THROUGH YOUR WEEKLY BLUEPRINT THAT YOU HAVE JUST CREATED. YOUR MASTERLIST NEEDS TO COVER ALL THE ACTIVITIES THAT MAKE UP THE CORE AREAS OF YOUR LIFE AND WORKING WEEK.

DO A BRAIN DUMP OF ABSOLUTELY EVERYTHING THAT YOU NEED TO DO TODAY, TOMORROW AND IN THE FORESEEABLE FUTURE.

KEEP ADDING TO THE LIST ++++

KEEP REVERTING BACK TO THE LIST

ONCE A WEEK, TRANSFER ITEMS FROM THIS ANOTHER LIST ONTO A LIST SPECIFICALLY DESIGNED FOR THE WEEK AND SCHEDULE THEM INTO YOUR CALENDAR.

IF ONCE A WEEK IS TOO SELDOM, DO A DAILY TRANSFER AND MAKE A DAILY TO DO LIST.

WHEN YOU FEEL OVERWHELMED, COME BACK TO YOUR LIST AND RE-ORIENTATE YOURSELF.

WHILE CREATING YOUR FIRST MASTER LIST CONSIDER LETTING GO OF ALL THE THINGS THAT YOU FEEL OBLIGED TO DO, BUT DON'T ACTUALLY NEED TO DO.

CONSIDER MAKING A SEPARATE NOT-TO-DO MASTER LIST.

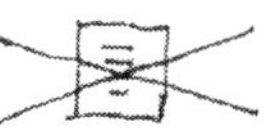

ADD ACTIVITIES TO YOUR LIST THAT INDULGE, GROW AND STRENGTHEN YOUR CREATIVITY.

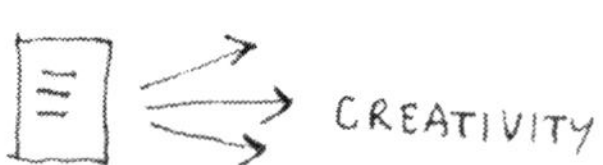

WHEN TRANSFERRING FROM YOUR MASTERLIST TO YOUR WEEKLY OR DAILY LIST, ENSURE THAT YOU SCHEDULE AT LEAST ONE CREATIVE ACTIVITY PER WEEK

26 •

CREATIVITY NEEDS DARK Places

"flat light is also light. it works, just differently"

Rochelle is elfin in every way: pointed little nose covered with freckles and a bob cut to her thin, straightened, strawberry blond hair that bounces with every step she takes. I stare at her wrists for an inordinate amount of time. The skin that covers the inner workings is translucent like curtain netting. Her bones seem brittle underneath and yet they move deftly as she clicks the back of the camera in the pitch darkness and removes the roll of film. It's a black and white film, 400 speed, textured and pearly. She motions towards Jenna and me, somewhat aggravated; we are both aware of the fact that she thinks she is doing us a favour, being here, on this sunny afternoon.

Her favourite subject is horses. She rides them, photographs them, grooms them. She agitates the developer tank, leaves it to rest. The darkness makes us speak in hushed tones, although there is no need. She speaks about Bristle, the horse she is breaking in with difficulty. Her voice has a sticky sweetness to it. That, coupled with her desire to sound English, makes her hard to listen to. She looks at me then: "Claire, he is feisty, like you, has a will of his own. Maybe you should come speak to him sometime—tell him that training is not a bad thing." I smile wryly. I know this is not meant as a compliment.

I look back to the developer tank, hoping that the next agitation is needed. I want the attention off me. She rattles the tank a little too vigorously and some fixer splashes out of the bottle balancing on the workbench. I watch breathlessly as she moves through a series of movements and agitations, arms criss-crossing and dipping as each image emerges

crisp and lucid, just like her. I watch those miniscule wrists at work again, clipping her horses onto the drying cables. Bristle does appeal to me. He has a sorrowful look in his eye, a broadness in his shoulders and the most magnificent curve in his back leading into a tail so vast and long that I imagine plaiting it.

Finally the hooter is heard from the far end of the pine trees, muffled by the thick blanket of needles that covers the parking area. Rochelle gathers her stuff hurriedly and looks at us with warning, icy eyes. "Don't damage my prints." The door clicks. We both exhale.

No more hushed whispers—just silence as Jenna and I settle into our own worlds. My work is moody, dark and reflective of the shadows that chase teenaged versions of me. I'm interpreting the darkness within, transferring it into ink that forms lines of shadow and light. My favourite days out with my camera are days where the light is flat. I don't understand why other photographers are always chasing the light. Flat light is also light. It works, just differently.

Some days I shoot colour film, cross-process it, wondering if life can work in the same way, if I can do things intended for other purposes and watch vibrancy emerge. On other days, most days in fact, I shoot black and white. I like the grain of 400 or 800 speed film. The clarity of 100 and 200 speed film is too crisp for my liking. The simplicity of grainy monotone works well with my raging hormones and inner anger. I shoot two shots on the same film strip, creating blurs that make no sense and perfect sense all at once.

Creating pictures that need second glances is an art. The average human on the street will pass them by, but people with some curiosity and sense of individuality will stop, look deeper and find their own interpretations in the blurred lines of reality that criss-cross before their eyes.

I move the roll of film out of the canister and into the dark room, counting as my fingers move from the edge of each slide to the next. From there I move to the developing tank, transferring my own agitation into the activity as I slightly sway the tank ensuring that all air bubbles are gone. I do this a few times before moving to the stop bath, to fixer, to water bath.

I watch with incredulity as each image emerges. Surfacing from the liquid is the object that I captured at a certain angle with a particular slant of light but in equal measure another image materialises, all its own making. This part of film processing always catches me by surprise. I can't control the outcome; I can navigate it through its watery birth, but ultimately the picture is what it is, not what I want it to be.

In pursuit of creativity:

1. What dark places have developed your creativity?
2. Take a walk and reflect back on the dark places in your past. What lessons can you glean and use in your creative work?
3. Create two columns. Label the one 'past' and the other 'lesson'. Free write for 10 minutes in bullet point form all that you thought about on your walk.

CREATIVITY
is ultimately
ALLOWING THE PICTURE
to be what it is,
NOT what I WANT
IT TO BE.

27 • COUNTING *five* Fingers

Creativity

needs

to

MASTER

loneliness

"more than anything I want it to end"

The swing slowly nudges back and forth. My toes create troughs in the dark red soil that gets deeper and deeper each time I push back and forth. I imagine a farm with long stretches of land that need to be watered with those big sprinklers that stretch and spray water like a controlled waterfall across everything. I imagine the trenches of water that pool and then seep in, just like in the garden where Granny planted the yellow and pink foxgloves.

Slanted light falls between the leaves, flashing in my eyes as I swing through. I squint my eyelids, then hold my hand up, inspecting the bumps formed by each small bone. I look deeply at the way my skin wraps itself around each shape, tightening and releasing in just the right places. I watch as the sun seeps through the holes that my fingers cannot fill.

Laughter erupts somewhere on the playground and I scan, trying to pinpoint where it comes from. I need to crane to see because I am hidden under a Jacaranda tree in full purple bloom. The laughter is coming from the sandpit. It always comes from that direction. That's where Kelly, Josey-Anne and Natasha play. John and Michael also play there. I was enjoying my farm dream, but now I'm staring back at the expanse of red, dry earth that forms my playground, once again reminded that it's breaktime and more than anything I want it to end. For now, though, I'm safe under the tree where the soil is soft and light slants in.

Mom and Dad don't know that I don't like coming to school, because I do like school; I just don't like breaktime. I like the stories that Mrs Dorset makes come alive with her moving hands and changing voices. I squeal with glee in art class when we hack shapes into potato bodies, dip them into paint and press them onto fresh paper,

leaving marks uniquely ours. I like constructive playtime, when I get to "cook" with plastic vegetables and mini pans. I set the table and tell my invisible friends to come to dinner. I like lying on my little mattress covered in squeaky plastic after lunch. I count to 50 and know that when I open my eyes, Dad will be walking up the corridor to take me home.

In primary school, break becomes a bit more tolerable because I can play soccer and rugby (to my mother's horror) and actually contribute to the game. My height, speed and carelessness about wearing a dress have something to do with this, but once I hit age twelve I realize that wearing a dress is actually about keeping your panties hidden and so rather than running at full speed, I find solace in Mrs Du Preez's classroom. She has interesting books about ethereal characters, and I find reasons to read them rather than be outside for break time. In high school, I spend my eighth-grade year drifting from group to group, never quite losing that sinking feeling when the ten o'clock bell rings. Each day I wait expectantly for the two-ten bell to ring, so I can leave for home and store up a reserve to face tomorrow all over again.

At age fifteen, I finally realise I don't have a strategy and that I need one. Quickly.

I start with Elmien, the Afrikaans girl who struggles with English. She has piercing blue eyes, inflamed skin, and one of her legs is very, very thin. I speak to her in Afrikaans and ask her if she wants to come and sit with me at breaktime. It's just the two of us for a few weeks. We fall into a comfortable pattern of spending those silly few minutes before the start of the school day chit-chatting and then break a couple of hours later becomes bearable, if not something to look forward to.

Bronwyn is next. She's slamming her locker this morning, skulking the corridor, making it nearly impossible for her wobbly suitcase on wheels to keep up with her. She's banging her big pencil box down. My hand touches her back and she mumbles something about that friendship being over. I ask if she wants to meet us at breaktime. She nods.

I find Emma in English class. Her words mesmerise me. She writes and keeps journals. She's crying because of a friendship gone wrong. I offer her a place until it's resolved. She comes, planning to leave, but never quite does.

Four years later, a few months before we will be leaving school, I find Georgia. Everyone has been whispering about her in hushed tones. She's been hospitalised for anorexia, though the diagnosis is inaccurate; her emaciated condition turns out to be caused by a life-threatening gluten intolerance. She's been part of the popular girls' group: the hockey stars, the netball stars, the swimmers. Something makes me think she doesn't feel so popular anymore. I invite her to our place: the little garden behind the science labs where we eat chocolate mousse straight from one big tub—that place where school became a happy place. She comes with her skeletal body and we embrace her with the fullness of our own.

It starts with counting five fingers on a swing. It ends with five friends.

IN Pursuit of CREATIVITY:

1. When have you Felt intense loneliness IN your Life?
2. What is your strategy to handle Loneliness?
3. Make a List of people who intrigue you. FIND WAYS TO BEFRIEND THEM.

"Each Day → IS AN EXPECTANT WAITING."

Creativity
needs
the
Giant
child
experience

"i tower over these little people as if i am a giant"

The chaotic mess of little urchins screech, splash, and dare each other to dive so that Miss Pam will shout at them. Pool noodles, towels, goggles, flip flops and clothes lie scattered around the rim of the pool. The huge floor-to-ceiling, three-storey glass window that looms over the shallow end of the water floods sunlight onto its surface, creating little diamonds I want to catch with a butterfly net. My mind starts racing: What the hell am I doing here? Why did I phone her five times and beg her to teach me? What was I thinking? I'm an adult and I've signed myself up for a toddler swimming class.

She looks at me, and I can see a wry smile playing at the corner of her mouth. I look ridiculous. I know it. I tower over these little people as if I am a giant. One of the little urchins starts counting all the people in the class: his designated duty and source of huge pride. This is a big responsibility. He taps each classmate on the head and counts loudly so all his friends know he is busy at work. He gets to me and his little hand hesitates, moving up my body but not able to reach my head. It moves slowly down, realising it can't tap my breasts and ends on my tummy, where it stays as he slowly turns to look at the teacher.

"Miss Pam, do I need to count this lady, too?"

"Yes, Paulie, she's part of your class; that's why she's standing on the side of the pool with all of you."

"But I can't tap her head to count her, Miss Pam."

"That's okay, Paulie. You can tap her tummy."

"Okay, Miss Pam. 'Number 22,'" he says bossily as he marches forward.

I might be six feet tall, but that means nothing in this water world. Pam sends them on their way and starts working with me on the side. Paulie takes great pride in knowing I am behind him in this process of paddles, strokes, kicks and breathing. He gets to warm up with the others while I get my head dunked under the water over and over again until Pam is certain that I can come up correctly for air and water. She keeps repeating this, telling me that the muscles in my neck are lifting up, as if I am going to drown. I need to relax and try and look at my legs and toes below the water, past my stomach. It takes great effort on my part to relax because it does feel as if I am going to drown and I really do need to come up for air more quickly than she is trying to train me to do. She keeps pushing my head down, holding it there, and bringing it up slowly. After what seems like five minutes, she announces that the lesson is over. I look at her incredulously and hear Paulie and Jacob laughing in the background.

She looks at me and says, "Well I can't be dunking your head for another thirty minutes, can I?" I'm dismissed and told that I passed the first lesson with flying colours. She will see me again in two days. So much for neck and back muscle strengthening after a car accident and repetitive physical therapy. I now have a delicious headache concocting itself in my neurons. I wonder if she will be seeing me back in two days when Paulie comes screeching past me. His hands land smack on my tummy. "Bye-bye Number 22. See you on Thursday." No backing out now, I think to myself.

On Thursday I return, towering like a beach umbrella next to little bottles of suntan lotion. I've been upgraded. I am allowed to do warm-up laps with the little urchins today. After ten minutes of that, I'm once again pulled aside. Today is hand- and arm-movement day. Pam is in the water with me showing me how my hand needs to cup inwards and pull down when it touches the surface of the water. She has all my weight propped up on her leg, which feels slightly awkward. My arm is being pulled back and then pushed forward at an unfamiliar angle. I can feel my nerves trying to adjust into new patterns of movement. They feel as awkward as I do.

I really should've chosen another gym for these lessons, I think to myself. Why did I choose the one gym where the rest of the workout area is built around the swimming pool? In most gyms, the pool is built in a separate area away from the weights, bikes and dance rooms. But not here. In this one, the entire gym looks down on twenty-three urchins and one towering grownup attending swim classes. Hindsight tells me this was a bad choice. Better think things through next time.

Pam is thankful, though. A month later she has to create two adult swim classes due to popular demand and repetitive questions by curious onlookers from the gym, asking if they, too, could join the swim class.

IN Pursuit of CREATIVITY:

1. WHEN have you LEARNT SOMETHING NEW AND gone through a period of embarrassment BECAUSE OF IT?
2. Make a LIST OF five things THAT you really want to LEARN TO DO PROPERLY, EVEN IF IT MEANS having to be a 'child' AGAIN.
3. Describe WHAT will be different WHEN you HAVE LEARNT THIS new skill.

CREATIVITY
NEEDS TO BECOME A
CHILD again.

11 ways to be a kid in ADULT skin

• 29

1. DO THINGS THAT CHILDREN DO

2. IMMERSE YOURSELF IN A SITUATION Rather THAN OBSERVING IT.

3. TAKE PART, BE A CONTRIBUTOR

4. FOCUS ON ONE THING THEN MOVE ONTO THE NEXT →

5. GET EXCITED ABOUT SMALL THINGS.

6. Express Emotions

7. TAKE YOUR TIME DOING THINGS

8. ASK MANY Questions

9. ASK MANY MORE Questions

10. LOSE YOURSELF IN THE PROCESS, FORGETTING THE OUTCOME.

11. START WITH WHAT YOU HAVE. DON'T ASK FOR THE PERFECT TOOLKIT OR LIST.

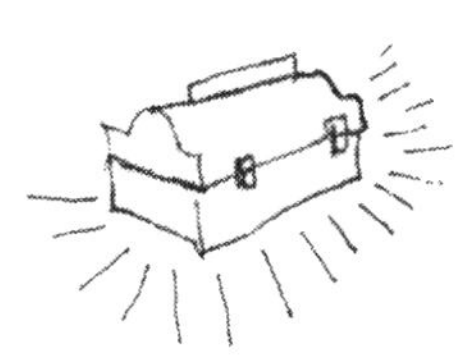

Creativity

NEEDS
TO
Drink
DEEPLY

"with mouths open wide, we gulp at the fresh warm liquid flooding our beings"

A spring wind, warm and cold all at once, whips around me, trying to shape my hair into the perfect ice-cream-cone coiffe. This shy season hides herself in Ireland, where I now live far from my South African childhood. Eventually spring arrives bearing gifts in profusion. Anne and I stand at the hedgerows, inspecting them meticulously, hoping to spot the first burst of green so we know spring is truly on the way and not planning to leave for a while. Down the road, Jamie and Aine chase each other with bare branches. They look back every now and then, willing Anne and me, the two slow adults, to hurry on up.

Just beyond the hedgerows, the woolly cows graze in fits. Head down, chew-chew-chew, look up. We try to speak cow language, exhaling soft, low moos. Sometimes our sounds resonate with the lumbering creatures and sleepy eyes look up and stare for a while.

Our boots are mucked up: manure, hay, rain all make for the perfect mush pile, ready to be shaped into any mould willing to accept it. The soles of our shoes fall prey. We keep walking towards the shed just ahead.

Jamie hears Freddy's bellow in the yard and races ahead, trying to tug Aine along. She resists, morphs into a ragdoll so his cajoling has little effect. He runs ahead, turns back and runs towards us to warm his hands in his mom's jacket pockets. The wind carries his voice as he runs away again: "Claire is going to meet Freddy. Claire is going to meet Freddy. Claire is going to meet Freddy."

Anne's laughter gurgles in my ears, mingles with the angry snorting of the bull as we near the shed.

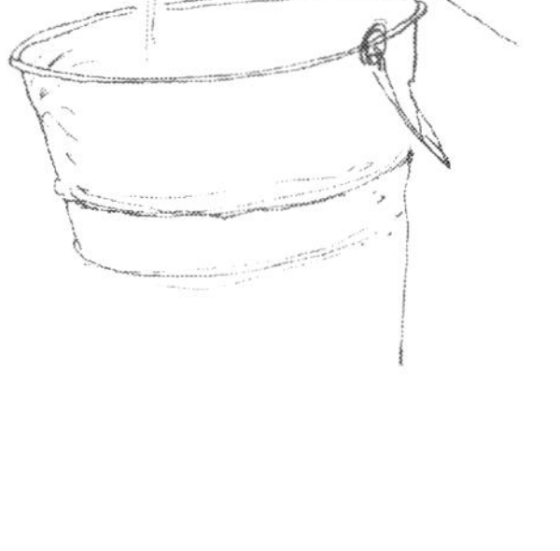

I turn the corner. Jamie is jumping up and down excitedly, inviting me to admire his big, proud and very hormonal bull.

I see the farmer and his cow instead.

Her udder is beautiful and full, oozing milk into a bucket. From the bucket, the white pearly liquid gets tipped into a large metallic urn.

I pull over a bucket lying on its side in the corner, tip it wrong side up, and perch myself on it. I watch as hands work at udder skin, pulling, tugging, and inching sideways to ensure the stream lands neatly in the bucket below—a hard labour of love for a very small return.

Jamie is looking for me. I see him peeking at me from underneath the udder. His face lights up as I beckon him closer. "Jamie, come look here what Uncle Dominique is doing. Look how he moves the udder to make sure all the milk comes out."

He leans up and whispers in my ear. "Come and see where all the milk goes, Claire."

A mischievous smile floods his eyes as he tugs at my hand. We go to the big tank where the milk is filling up, spilling and splashing about.

I pick him up. We both take hold of the hose. With mouths open wide, we gulp at the fresh warm liquid flooding our beings.

IN PURSUIT OF CREATIVITY:

1. What hoses do you need to open up wide in your life?
2. What moments in your life STAND OUT AS OUT-OF-THE-ordinary?
3. Think about and list all the times you have restrained yourself from being spontaneous. How did you feel afterwards?

"Creativity has a thirst that needs to be quenched."

31 •

Creativity
Needs
TIME
to simmer

"the story of a life that paints a door blue is one I would like to hear"

The brightness of fire-engine red lures me back to this town again and again. Most return for the river that flows widely through the stone buildings and curves around the shape of the hill up ahead. Or they come for the pub: that place where music seems to secure itself into the walls, echoing silently long after the instruments have been laid down. Something about the stonework in the village, offset by the brightness of the red, captivates me in the afternoon sun—especially five o' clock sun, the kind that illuminates everything in its path.

I walk around the house with its roughened, white finish that looks as if the painter used an old brush with loose bristles that tangled in the paint, leaving lumps along the wall. It is the Cape Cod blue that stops me. I crane my neck, standing on tiptoes outside the window to see if anyone is home. Mom taught me that it's rude to be a "Peeping Tom," but I cannot help myself today. This little cottage needs my attention. It tells me so. I walk back to the door to admire the shocking pink fuchsias with their purple earrings that dangle and sway in the wind.

Words I scrawled across a journal page come rushing into my mind as I stand tentatively, hoping that the door might just open itself...

> "they just keep finding me. these blue doors. i think i might just have to knock on one someday. i quite fancy the idea of asking for the person who answers, to tell me a story. anything really. but a story of a life that paints a door blue, is one i would like to hear."

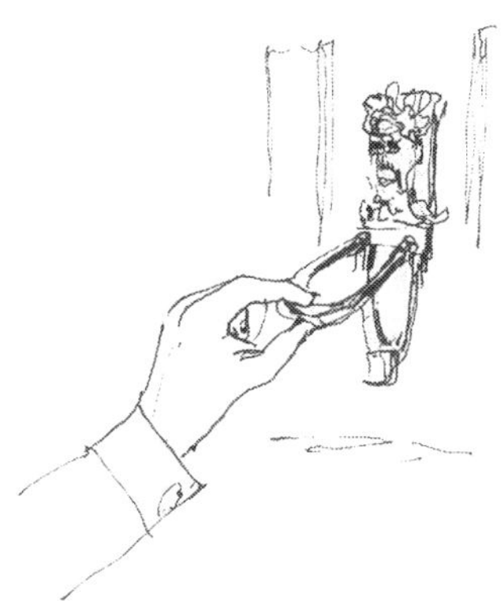

I cannot see movement, but then again the window lords over a spare terracotta-tiled passageway, leaving me guessing as to the innards of this home. I raise my hand to knock, but hesitate. I let it hang limp at my side, turn to look at the river, turn back again, and raise my hand... but cannot knock.

My life moves to Dublin. I leave the red brick town behind and with it the blue door and its unknown inhabitants. The idea of knocking at a blue door lingers. My courage is incubating.

I do nothing about it for a few months. I find an office in town. Each day I walk past colourful doors. The blue doors catch my eye most. I like the variety of shades in blue. Blue seems more expansive than other colours, more inviting somehow.

On a grey day, rain splattering around me, I raise my hand and knock on a soft blue, almost grey, door that takes me back to Ramelton where I first found that Cape Cod door.

Stories unfold. Invites back are extended. Tea is poured. Lasagne is made. Blue doors become green doors, become yellow doors, become red doors.

IN Pursuit of CREATIVITY:

1. WHAT really intrigues you and keeps catching your attention?
2. what holds you back from exploring it?
3. Take the first step towards exploring this thing that intrigues you so. Go OUT and do it as soon as you can.

32 •

The Abandoned House

CREATIVITY NEEDS mystery???

"you're going to fall through the floor boards!"

The gusty morning whips through my cardigan, pulling it away from my body. I tug it back, wrap it tighter around me, close the window and turn up the heat. The clouds disperse and cluster in the sky. The fields are velveteen green. We are lost but happy to be so. A car travels ahead of us at a distance. We pass a ramshackle house that is evidently no longer in use; the lace curtains in front of the windows catch my eye.

"Stop. Stop. I have to get photos of this."

I stand back at first, taking in the beauty of the lifeless skeletal structure before me. I notice the teapot in the grass. I step forward gingerly, realising there is a story here. A story that needs unravelling.

I peer into the windows and gasp. A full house, time warped from yesteryear, stares back at me. It is as if a loving wife polished her husband's shoes and laid them in front of the fire. A tea cup rests on the table in its chipped saucer. I desperately try to piece together why all the remains of a well-off life have stayed behind, why a home that was once beautiful has been left to ruin and rot—to brave the elements and vandals. There are no locks on the door, and my heart says, "Go in." My husband, Calvin, whispers behind me that I am trespassing.

Before I can step in, the car that was ahead of us has parked alongside the house. A man in his mid-seventies with an unshaven face, muddy boots and an easy smile opens the car window and greets us in a distinct Donegal dialect. Calvin inquires as to whether he is from the area, hoping that no explanation for his trespassing wife will need to be given. He eagerly replies that he is and asks whether or not we want to know the story behind the house. My smile belies my curiosity.

"Well, of course, Lass. Come on in."

Mr and Mrs O'Connor lived in the tidy little house for many years. They passed away with absolutely no relations to take care of their affairs, and the house stands as an eerie testament to a life lived with no legacy. Curiosity dangles on the tip of my tongue but I bite it back, not asking how they died. These rural Irish live in the shadows of superstition; I don't want to unsettle something I shouldn't. Shoes remain tucked beside the hearth. Her purse lies on the kitchen table as if she came in yesterday from town and left it just there. The fireplace holds logs and ash in its bosom and the kitchen window is ajar, revealing a table set for breakfast. A sewing kit is strewn across a dresser, attesting to the toll time has taken on this abandoned beauty. Mrs O'Connor was such a pedantic woman that when the farmers would walk past with their sheep to put them through the dipping pen, she would constantly sweep the gravel to ensure that no marks from sheep hooves would remain to ruin her perfect little house and driveway. "Pleasant enough, though," Mr Kelly remarks.

All the while I eye the passageway and the rotting staircase, giving way under the weight of time.

Somewhere behind me, Calvin warns, "No, Claire. You're going to fall through."

Curiosity prevents me from looking back.

"Naaah lass, he's just in love. You come on over and climb onto the old man's back. He will lift you up to the parts that aren't rotten and then you can explore upstairs."

"Claire, you're going to fall through the floorboards!"

I'm up on the landing, halfway into the first room, happily taking photos of every object I would rather take home with me than leave behind. I carefully step into the second room, Calvin's words ringing in my mind. The rotten wood starts giving way, millimeter by millimeter—

each creak amplified by the expectant silence of both Mr Kelly and Calvin below.

I try to throw my weight out of the door, seconds too late. Everything creaks and moans beneath my weight as the floorboards give way and my legs dangle from the landing into the kitchen. I am suspended between two floors of an abandoned house: a rare and privileged position in which to find myself.

I start giggling when Calvin's voice breaks the reverie: "Darn it! I told you not to do it! Now look!"

Mr Kelly looks up at my dangling legs, shrugs off the statement, and says mischievously, "Naah, aai the lass she be a wee bit ok."

Mr Owen Kelly ("O.K." as he now calls himself), a disgruntled Calvin, a giggling me and a bleating sheep share the sunshine outside the house. We are about to leave when Mr O.K. decides he is not quite ready to let us go and that a further tour of the farm is needed. We climb the hill together as his lilts take me back to another year, another life...

IN PURSUIT OF CREATIVITY:

1. What mysteries do you want to unravel?
2. How do you go about finding mystery, and then exploring it?
3. Without thinking too long and hard, make a list of all the things from childhood up until now in your journey that have really piqued your interest. Do you see recurring patterns?

"Curiosity and creativity need to meet for tea more regularly."

• 33

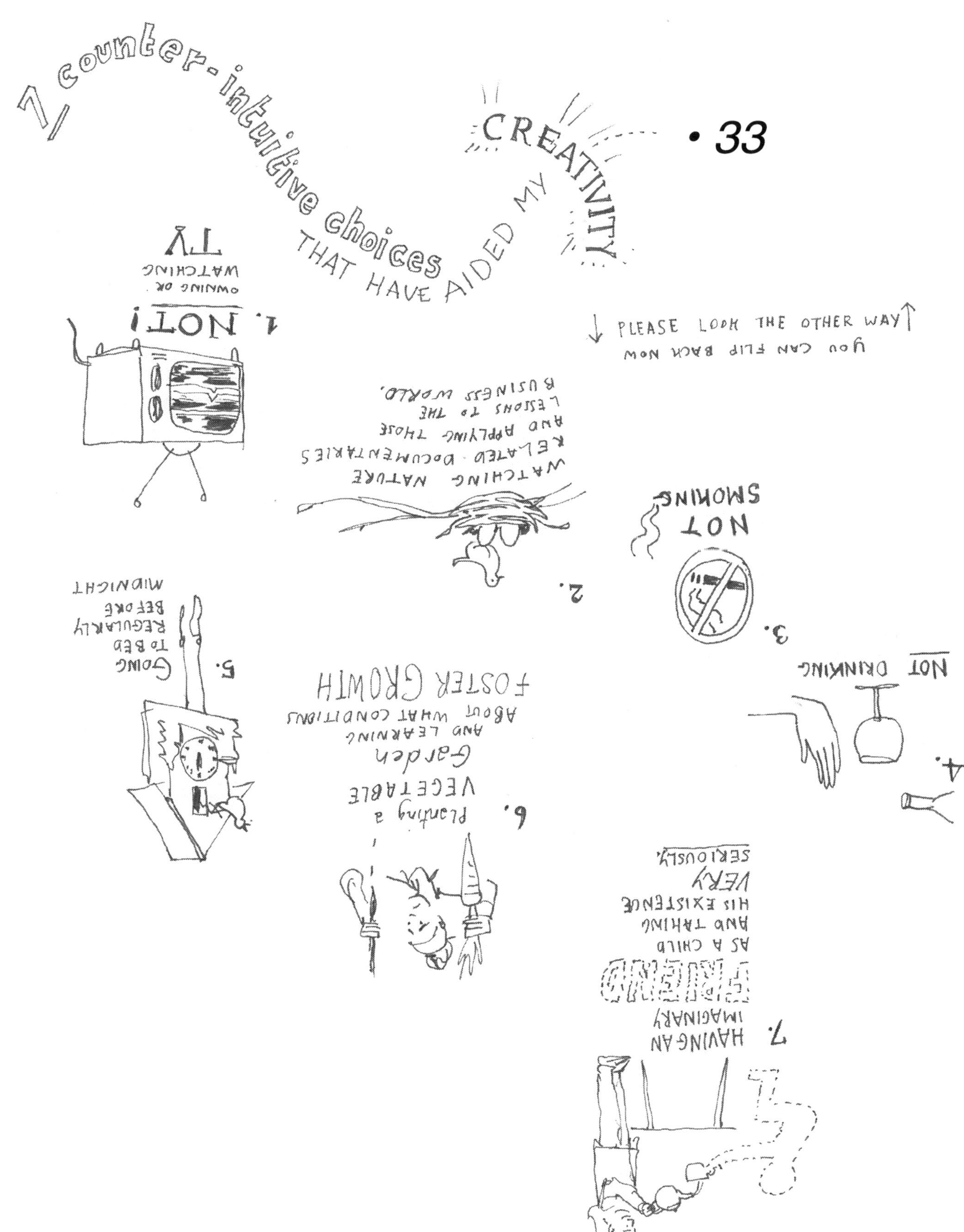

7 counter-intuitive choices THAT HAVE AIDED MY CREATIVITY
↓ PLEASE LOOK THE OTHER WAY ↑
YOU CAN FLIP BACK NOW
1. NOT!
OWNING OR WATCHING TV
2. WATCHING NATURE RELATED DOCUMENTARIES AND APPLYING THOSE LESSONS TO THE BUSINESS WORLD.
3. NOT SMOKING
4. NOT DRINKING
5. GOING TO BED REGULARLY BEFORE MIDNIGHT
6. Planting a VEGETABLE Garden AND LEARNING ABOUT WHAT CONDITIONS FOSTER GROWTH
7. HAVING AN IMAGINARY FRIEND AS A CHILD AND TAKING HIS EXISTENCE VERY SERIOUSLY.

34 • A tale of two Chickens

Creativity
NEEDS
TO
Recognize
Life

"i make the mistake of naming them"

Calvin arrives, flustered and agitated. The creatures are flapping about. He wants them out of the back seat—fast.

I make the mistake of naming them. I really shouldn't do it. The ones who know from years of hard-earned experience all warn me; but, being me, I do it anyway. I name them from a story that my mom told me, which I vaguely recall; then, I also name them according to their behaviour, which is too evident to be ignored.

"Hardy" is a girl, but as feisty and boyish as the day is long. I am sure that her deepest desire is to be a bomber pilot because the girl attempts flight around the garden all day with her wings spread out, little feet racing at full tilt towards the garden fence. She comes to a screeching halt just before her head collides with it, chickening out quite literally at the last minute. I stand at the kitchen window watching her, wishing I could buy her a pair of bomber glasses. She would look ridiculously sassy!

Timid Laurel soaks up love at every opportunity. Her feathered body hunkers down low every morning as soon as she hears my farm boots scuffling on the gravel path that leads to her coop. I can hear her soft landing from atop the perch and the way she scuffles down into the hay, waiting for her morning scratch.

Donegal has a way of being cold year round, so my gloved hands struggle with the small lock that is icy at six o'clock in the morning. I wiggle and wrangle it, finally sliding it loose. The wooden door opens an inch or two, and I peep in only to find myself face-to-face with Hardy, eager to escape her palace immediately.

And believe me, it is a palace. Compared with the living standards of every other chicken in the world, this coop is no mere coop. It is made

for eight, but houses two. The hay is replaced weekly, the poop is scooped daily, the water is freshened twice daily, the food is brought on time for every meal, and yet this dear old girl just wants out.

In the harshest of snow, my scuffling boots are her call to inspect the outside world for one more day. Exploration awaits beyond this door. Of that, she is sure. Laurel, on the other hand, needs coaxing. Her hunkering down is my signal for the routine morning scratch. I stroke her little orange-and-dapple-brown feathers while she cocks her head to one side. She patiently sits and watches everything I do, following my hands from one side of the coop to the other.

One day a badger comes. Laurel hides. Hardy tries to destroy him, tapping into her skills as a bomber pilot. Hardy becomes badger supper. I cry as I clear the drive of feathers and innards and little claw feet. Laurel cries, too. She lays a soft shell egg the next morning. I hold her and cry some more.

IN PURSUIT OF CREATIVITY:

1. HAVE YOU CONSIDERED THAT LIFE TEEMS IN THE UNLIKELIEST OF PLACES?
2. WHERE HAVE YOU POSSIBLY OVERLOOKED LIFE?
3. TAKE AN EVERYDAY OBJECT AND PERSONIFY IT IN AN ART FORM OF YOUR CHOICE.

"IN *tenderness creativity finds* A *texture*."

35 •

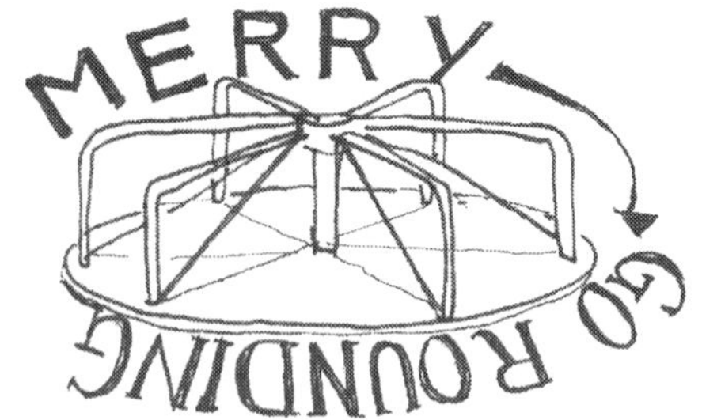

Creativity
Needs
to
Network

"together their hands take hold of the metal bars and their bodies will the piece of equipment forward"

The map is all frumpled and creased, unable to return to its original neat fold-me-up position. It is dog-eared and red-pen-marked. The red marks are squiggles and dots that indicate roads travelled and destinations where the view has been taken in. In some places town names have been scribbled over with "stunning!" and "steep cliffs." It hugs the door of the car, bulging out of its compartment, begging for yet another adventure.

Today the sun is rippling through the ever-present clouds and all I want to do is play. I check the map for a side road I once spotted but didn't have time to explore. I turn the car in that direction.

I find the road but then discover the park, sloped on a grassy hill at the base of a pine forest. From the basket swing, I can see all the way out to Lambay Island.

I arch my back as far back as it will go, taking in the cobalt of the sky, the slate of the clouds, the rust of bark in my line of curvature. Somewhere mid-arc, I notice two little pairs of legs marching towards the merry-go-round in the distance.

Little Mr Plaid Shirt climbs onto the merry-go-round and stands, waiting. Little Mr Button-Up observes, and then also climbs on. Both stand, looking at each other. Together their hands take hold of the metal bars and their bodies will the piece of equipment forward. It goes nowhere. They stop wishing, look at each other. The one gets off and with all his might and little arms, starts pushing the structure forward.

He makes little progress. He kicks at the gravel. Once, twice, eleven times. Slowly he gains momentum. The structure starts moving and then starts spinning faster and faster. He jumps on, out of breath. Laugher erupts. Round and round they go.

Little Miss Cotton Dress on the balance beam looks over, asks her dad to take her there. Little Mr Thomas Tank Engine stops building a wood pile under a tree and stares in their direction. Little Miss Pigtails is tugging her mother's hand impatiently, willing her away from her comfortable seat on the swing.

Oblivious to the attention they are gaining, the original two boys keep spinning. The merriness starts slowing down, and only once they are at a near standstill do they realise that three other kids want to join in the fun.

I think back to my own childhood park experiences. The merry-go-round was by far my favourite piece of equipment. Still is.

Little Mr Plaid Shirt and Little Mr Button-Up are shrieking in the distance again. I see they have now cajoled Little Miss Pigtails and Little Mr Thomas Tank Engine into spinning them 'round and 'round.

It all makes sense. Swings are nice but merry-go-rounds are just that: merry. They bring friends along on the ride and they pick up some extras along the way.

I get back into the car, laughter still ringing in my ears, pull out the map and mark in bold red pen around the area of the park: Merry-go-rounds teach me how to network.

Later that night over pasta with peas and mint, I explain to my own very best merry-go-round friend that I learned all about networking by watching *spin* from the swings.

"Oh, really now, did you?"

"Yes. Really."

"How did this happen?"

"Well, you see, it started with this little boy in a plaid shirt who convinced his friend to merry-go-round and it took a while for them to gain momentum, but when they did, the spinning started and then before they knew it, a crowd had gathered..."

"It's all in the gaining momentum, then?"

"Yes, and it's all about creating the merriness..."

IN PURSUIT OF CREATIVITY:

1. What do everyday activities teach you about networking and building relationships?
2. How do you intentionally network to expand your reach and your contacts?
3. THINK carefully about how you build networks and relationships with new people in your life. Is there something that you can take from the merry-go-round concept to improve how you interact?

"Happiness AND TEAMWORK make for creative SOLUTIONS."

Creativity
Needs
STRANGERS

"the act of listening is about more than hearing"

The bridge is wide, generously so. It curves upward at its center the way a breast would. I want to see to the other side but I can't because the curve swallows the picture before me, calling me across. I wonder if this seduction is part of the architectural plan. I put one foot in front of the other and start making my way over. My natural inclination is to stride forward without looking around. I slow myself down, taking London in. I look down and follow the reflections of light as they play hopscotch on the water. Then I hear it briefly, look up but cannot locate it. I dismiss it as my imagination. The expansiveness of the bridge engages the adventure-seeker in me. I give in, allowing the dreams to run rife in my mind like sugarcane burning. Caution caged, I'm open to risk. I stand still and close my eyes. I incline my ears and hear it again, ever so softly. Without seeing, I imagine the fingers picking at the neck of the instrument. I see the callouses, hard from many hours of plucking. I am easily enticed. I follow.

I see him before he sees me. I slow down and listen. Something about the combination of his plucking appeals to me. It is off-beat and disconcerting in a comforting way. It is new, fresh.

He looks up, his dreads falling across his eyes. He looks down, not wanting to lose concentration. I wait, hesitating, until he realises that I'm not going to walk away. He looks up and I step right up to him, motion to the vast spaces around him, his guitar case and his woollen sweater that lie across the cold cement between us.

Again, I hesitate. My heart tugs at me to just sit down. My head tells me that I am being weird, that this is not socially acceptable

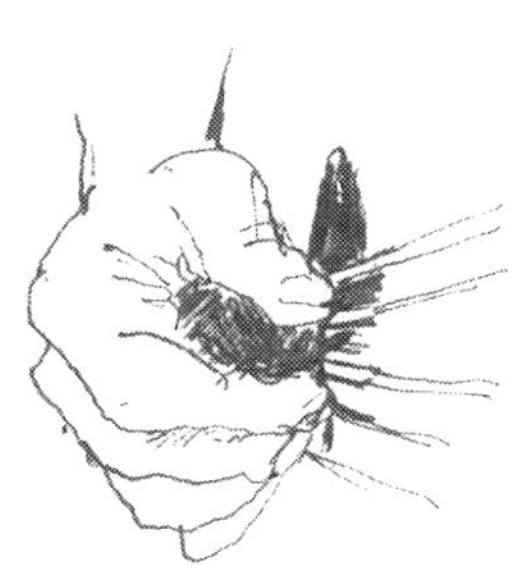

behaviour. The minor notes that he collects and re-births with those nimble hands of his have captivated me.

His head nudges right: no words are needed in this exchange. I settle down, prop my bag into the small of my back to ease the coldness of the cement. I close my eyes, lean my head against the railing, and inhale deeply the London smog.

Closing my eyelids, settling my racing mind, his music burrows into my being, courting me gently. I hear how his left hand flirts with his right: the one mysteriously disappearing before the other and then reappearing to make itself visible. He plucks, strokes, strums and beats with heartbeats that make his hands and heart collide.

Dusk becomes night; smog fades into low-hanging mist. The fall crispness descends. I wonder if his strumming would sound different under warmer skies, barer skin. Do we listen with more than the tiny bones in our ears? The bridge that carried me to him stretches before us now as if to Terabithia. It holds possibility, stretching beyond the immediate vision, curving as all good bridges do, as all realities should.

Courtesy says to drop a few coins into the open guitar case. I reach for my purse. My hand hesitates. I withdraw it. He senses my conundrum and shakes his head, willing my hand away from where it is placed. I want to give, but I can't. This was not a monetary exchange.

I gently tuck my hair behind my ears, get up. He looks at me and a slow, sad smile forms in the edges of his lips. I walk back to where I came from. His fingers continue weaving hearts together.

IN PURSUIT OF CREATIVITY:

1. WHAT do you really want to DO BUT WORRY WHETHER IT IS SOCIALLY ACCEPTABLE?
2. HOW DO you FEEL ABOUT talking to strangers?
3. MAKE a bullet point list about ALL THE KINDS OF PEOPLE IN YOUR WORK AND HOME VICINITY. THEN note down what intrigues you ABOUT THESE PEOPLE.

"Sometimes creativity requires ~~NO~~ ← WORDS →"

37 • 13 Actions / Attitudes that have proven worthwhile in my Creativity Toolbox

1. AUDACITY

2. OUTSPOKENESS ABOUT THINGS THAT RILE ME UP

3. RELENTLESS QUESTIONING

4. RETURNING TO A MATTER TO DISCUSS IT TO CONCLUSION, EVEN WHEN THE CONVERSATION GETS HEATED OR IS TENSE AT TIMES

5. LEARNING NEW SKILLS EVERY YEAR THAT ARE FAR OUTSIDE OF MY COMFORT ZONE

COMFORT ZONE

6. INSATIABLE CURIOSITY ABOUT OTHER PEOPLE'S STORIES.

7. INSATIABLE CURIOSITY FOR THE LITERAL PATHS I HAVE NOT EXPLORED.

8. OVERCOMING MY FEAR OF HEIGHTS ONCE AND AGAIN AND AGAIN

9. INSATIABLE CURIOSITY ABOUT DIFFERENT LANGUAGES, CULTURES, RELIGIONS, POLITICAL SYSTEMS AND ECONOMIES

10. FALLING OFF MY MOUNTAIN BIKE INNUMERABLE TIMES

11. ASKING FOR PERMISSION EVEN WHEN THE ODDS ARE STACKED VERY HIGH AGAINST ME.

PLEASE? ODDS

12. MAKING BOLD STATEMENTS JUST TO TEST REACTIONS.

13. STARTING DEBATES BECAUSE DIVERGENT VIEWS ARE HEALTHY

• 38

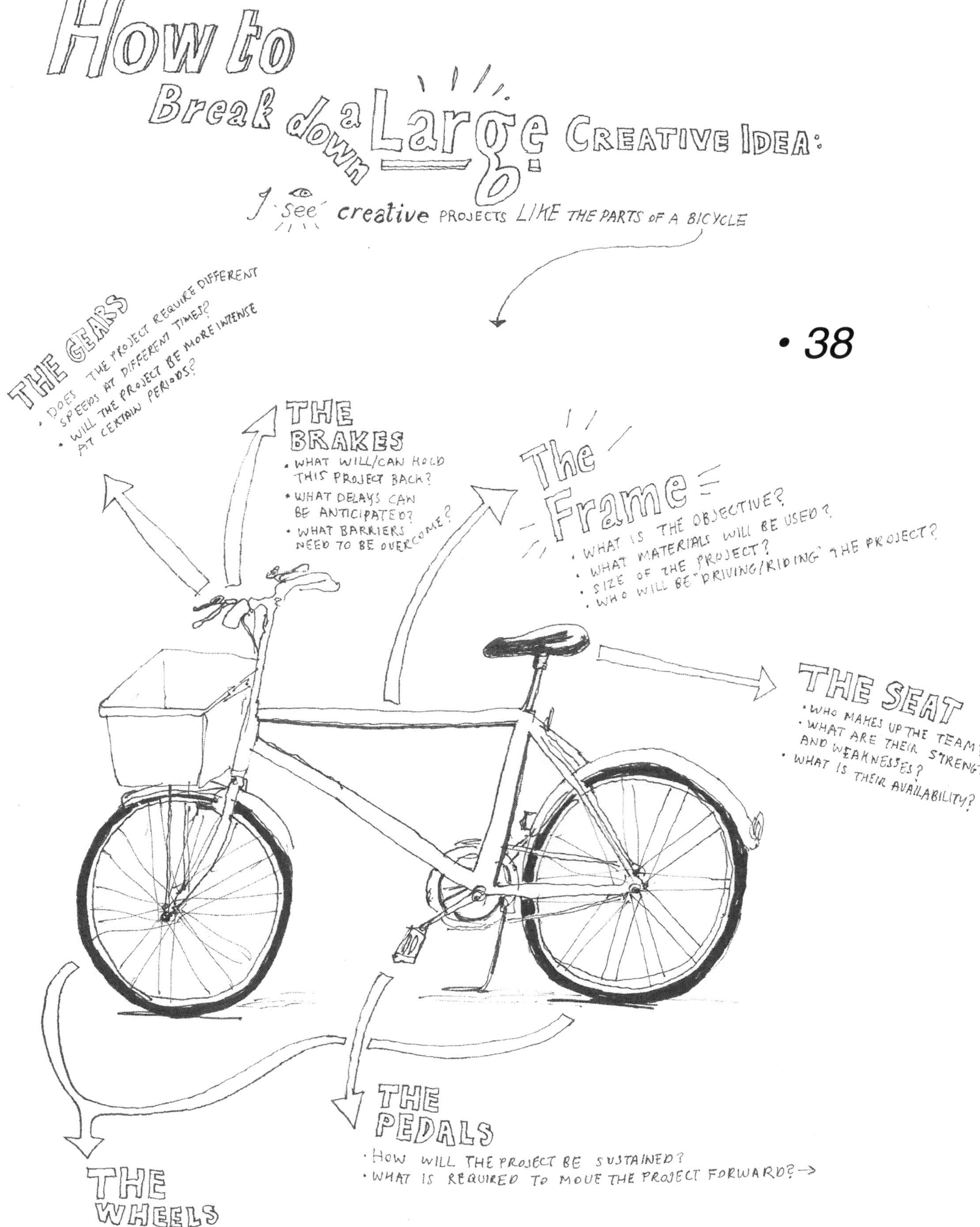

• WHAT IS MY MOTIVATION FOR DOING THIS PROJECT?
• IS IT WORK THAT FALLS INTO THE PASSION CATEGORY OR IS IT "PAY THE BILLS" WORK?
• HOW DOES IT FEED INTO MY LARGER GOALS?
• HOW DOES IT ADVANCE MY WORK AND CREATIVE LIFE AS A WHOLE?

39 • And So it Goes...

WHERE creativity is found: in that beautiful, brilliant space CALLED → being

The life lesson book/journal now lives in my handbag most of the time. It gets stuffed into my travel bag when we go away. It sometimes rides along in my backpack when I'm mountain-biking. When at home it travels between the bathroom, the study, the bedside table and the kitchen. Oh, and I definitely can't forget the daybed. Many lessons get noted in the afternoon sun while I'm lying there. I penned lesson #742 this morning while editing this manuscript. Someone gave me a sticker once. I generally throw those types of things away but I thought the words belonged inside the book so I stuck it on the back cover. It reads: "sharing is sexy."

My dad kept a biscuit tin with all his love letters from all his girlfriends through the years. I remember feeling like a little girl excitedly ripping open a cardboard box of surprises on her birthday when he shared it with me. I remember feeling closer to him because I saw a side of him that had been hidden from my view until that moment.

I often think of this when I journal and pen life lessons. I wonder what my children and my grandchildren and possibly even their children will take away from these lessons that I'm learning right now. Will it help them to connect their own selves, as fragments of their family history and lineage emerge before their eyes? Will it make them a little wiser? Spare them heartache or provide a way through?

I'll never know. But I can write it in the meantime.

So can you.

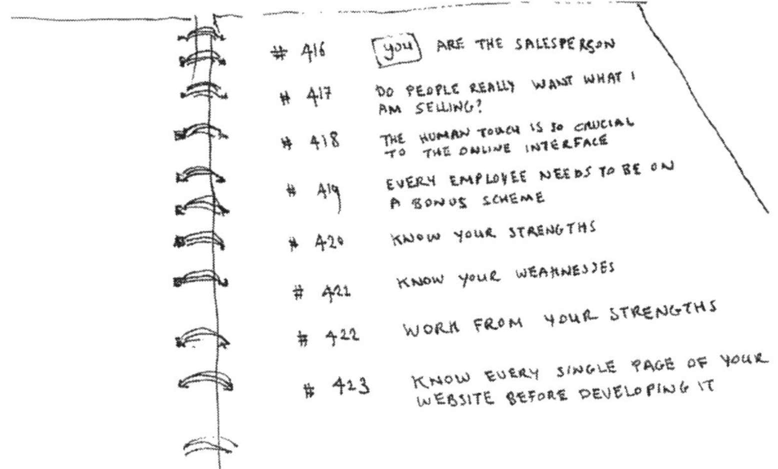

Dictionary of Terms

busker • British: a person who makes money by singing, dancing, acting, etc, in public places, as in front of theatre queues

chakalaka • South African vegetable relish, usually spicy

cupboard • a closet

hooter • a person or thing that hoots; British-a car horn

Marmite • British-trademark: a yeast and vegetable extract used as a spread, flavouring, etc.

oom • South African title of respect used to address an elderly man [Afrikaans: literally, uncle]

pip • a small seed, especially of a fleshy fruit, as an apple or orange

Sotho • a group of closely-related Bantu languages spoken in Lesotho and South Africa; any of the Sotho languages, especially Sesotho; also called Basuto, a member of any of a cluster of linguistically- and culturally-related Bantu-speaking peoples of southern Africa, including the Tswana

tannie • South African title of respect used to refer to an elderly woman [Afrikaans; literally: aunt]

tokoloshe • in Bantu folklore, a malevolent mythical manlike animal of short stature; also called *tikoloshe*

(All terms based on dictionary.com definitions, except for *chakalaka* which is from thefreedictionary.com)

Helpful Apps, Tools, and Practices

any.do is a playful phone, desktop and web task-list app that helps you plan your day. You can see your tasks within your calendar and set reminders—even set recurring tasks. It also has speech recognition.

Artist Date is a practice developed by Julia Cameron. Once a week, you set aside two hours to do something outside work or home. It should be fun and exploratory—anything from going to a museum, to hiking a trail, or checking out a new place to get coffee. Go alone. Go without agenda.

Evernote is a phone, desktop and web app that allows you to capture notes from anywhere. The notes can be audio, image, or text based. It is an electronic journal, if you will. Individual notes can also be clustered into notebooks and tagged for easy searching.

Goal Wall is a visual representation of the areas that make up your life. It is effective because it's a constant reminder of what you are aiming towards—even more effective when coupled with a Weekly Blueprint to ensure that you not only dream, but get things done about those dreams. A good goal wall should include:

1. Physical Goals
2. Mental/Education Goals
3. Relational Goals
4. Spiritual/Quiet Time Goals
5. Cultural Goals
6. Work/Business Goals
7. Hobby/Extramural Goals

Quiet Time is a period of time set apart, anywhere from fifteen minutes to an hour, where you perhaps sit outside with a cup of something hot to drink and simply do nothing. If you aren't liking the weather outside, you could sit quietly in a chair and let your thoughts disappear or drift.

Wunderlist is a phone, desktop and web app that allows you to create tasks and sub tasks, assign them to people, add due dates, mark them as complete and activate them again afterwards if necessary. It is intuitive and very easy to use. It works well for individuals and teams.

Also from T. S. Poetry Press

Rumors of Water: Thoughts on Creativity & Writing, by L.L. Barkat (twice named a Best Book of 2011)

A few brave writers pull back the curtain to show us their creative process. Annie Dillard did this. So did Hemingway. Now L.L. Barkat has given us a thoroughly modern analysis of writing. Practical, yes, but also a gentle uncovering of the art of being a writer.

— Gordon Atkinson, author *Turtles All the Way Down*

Booked: Literature in the Soul of Me, by Karen Swallow Prior

Prior movingly and honestly tells a compelling story of self-discovery through some of the greatest books ever written.

—Eric Metaxas, author of *New York Times* bestseller *Bonhoeffer: Pastor, Martyr, Prophet, Spy*

The Whipping Club, by Deborah Henry (an Oprah selection)

Multi-layered themes of prejudice, corruption and redemption with an authentic voice and swift, seamless dialogue. A powerful saga of love and survival.

—*Kirkus Reviews* (starred review)

T. S. Poetry Press titles are available through online vendors, in e-book and print editions. Print editions are also available through Ingram.

tspoetry.com

Made in the USA
Charleston, SC
15 March 2014